DIGITAL INCLUSION

DIGITAL INCLUSION

Measuring the Impact of Information and Community Technology

Edited by
Michael Crandall
and
Karen E. Fisher

asis&t
ASIST Monograph Series

Published on behalf of the
American Society for Information Science and Technology by

Information Today, Inc.
Medford, New Jersey

First printing, 2009

Digital Inclusion: Measuring the Impact of Information and Community Technology

Library of Congress Cataloging-in-Publication Data

Digital inclusion : measuring the impact of information and community technology / edited by Michael Crandall and Karen E. Fisher.
p. cm.
Includes bibliographical references and index.
ISBN 978-1-57387-373-4
1. Online social networks. 2. Internet--Social aspects. I. Crandall, Michael, 1948- II. Fisher, Karen E., 1966-
HM742.D54 2009
302.30285--dc22

2009029105

President and CEO: Thomas H. Hogan, Sr.
Editor-in-Chief and Publisher: John B. Bryans
Managing Editor: Amy M. Reeve
ASIST Monograph Series Editor: Samantha Hastings
Associate Editor: Claire Connell
VP Graphics and Production: M. Heide Dengler
Book Designer: Kara Mia Jalkowski
Cover Designer: Denise Erickson
Copyeditor: Dorothy Pike
Proofreader: Barbara Brynko
Indexer: Beth Palmer

Contents

PART 3: A FRAMEWORK FOR MEASUREMENT

Introduction

Michael Crandall and Karen E. Fisher

Digital inclusion is the rallying cry of the twenty-first century. Beyond access to computers and the internet for all, regardless of physical, cognitive or financial ability, the phrase "digital inclusion" signifies technological literacy and the ability to access relevant online content and services. Despite the tremendous wealth of American society and the numbers of people with computers and online access, significant pockets of the population remain at a disadvantage. Around the world, the situation is graver, as larger disparities exist among those who have the opportunity to use technology in ways that can benefit their lives and those who do not. A parallel concern is that tools are frequently lacking for effectively communicating how digital inclusion can be a powerful mechanism for affecting positive change in the lives of individuals, as well as entire families, villages, and countries.

This book is about digital inclusion in Washington State, how the Communities Connect Network mobilized to make a long-lasting difference in the lives of many people and gained the attention of policy makers to enact a law recognizing that impact. It is the story of community coming together: non-government organizations, municipal and state government, a foundation, and universities—each contributing its best to ensure that digital inclusion is occurring to wide effect.

On March 31, 2008, Washington State Governor Christine Gregoire signed Engrossed Second Substitute Senate Bill 6438 (see Appendix A) into law as Chapter 262 of the Laws of 2008 for Washington State. This law, for the first time ever, defines community technology in the state of Washington, making community technology programs eligible for state funding and providing recognition of the contributions they have made over the years to the individuals, families, and communities they serve within the state. The bill also provided $500,000 in state funds to assist community technology organizations in Washington achieve their missions over the following year.

At heart, this book: 1) provides a picture of the challenges in describing and measuring the impact community technology has had across the state of Washington, and 2) shares an evaluation approach, coined the Situated Logic Model, for communicating the impacts of digital inclusion programs, especially for understanding work with similar challenges. In this vein, we discuss the results of a two-year study conducted by the University of Washington Information School, and some of the steps taken to formalize and communicate the study results in a way that helped to achieve the remarkable results in the legislative arena.

This study was part of a much larger statewide movement, the Communities Connect Network, intended to bring community technology organizations together in the state of Washington, through training, education, and mobilization. The journey to the signing of the law is a story in itself, narrated briefly in Chapter 2, and could provide a significant case study in grass-roots organizing and advocacy. We hope that this story, and the intellectual underpinnings that provided the framework for the impact analysis, will provide insights into approaches that may be useful for others working in this area and a foundation for future work that can build on the lessons learned in this effort.

Two approaches were used to gather the information that this book will explore: a statewide telephone survey of the more than 200 community technology programs that were identified during the early stages of the project (Part 1), and case studies of seven organizations to better understand their impacts on individuals, families, and communities (Part 2). Both of these data-gathering activities were underlain by an examination of current approaches to measuring impact, resulting in the development of the Situated Logic Model framework discussed in Part 3. This framework should provide a model that others can use to conduct similar investigations and build on for future work. The results and findings are oriented toward those who are practicing in the field but grounded in academic research; both professionals and researchers should find something of value in the chapters that follow.

While this book focuses primarily on the research that was conducted with the community technology centers studied by the University of Washington, it is only one part of the statewide effort that resulted in the successful outcome. Six organizations played key roles in this effort: Washington State University's Center to Bridge the Digital Divide (cbdd.wsu.edu), the City of Seattle's Community Technology Program (www.seattle.gov/tech), Stone Soup (www.nwstonesoup.org), One Economy (www.one-economy.com), NPower Seattle (www.npowerseattle.org), and the University of Washington's Information School (www.ischool.washington.edu). Even more important were the scores of community technology programs in the state that participated in the training, capacity building events, legislative hearings, and grass-roots activities that ultimately provided the voices that resulted in the success of the bill. One of the strongest lessons to take away from this success is that it takes voices united in an effective organization to make a difference.

Finally, without the vision, leadership, and financial support of the Bill & Melinda Gates Foundation, none of this would have been possible. Its commitment to moving responsibility for success onto the shoulders of those who are doing the work, and making sure that the resources and tools that are necessary for the transition from support to ownership are available, provides a wonderful example for those funding organizations seeking to make real change in a community.

Part 1

Setting the Stage—Technology in the Community

CHAPTER 1

What Is Community Technology?

Michael Crandall and Karen E. Fisher

This book is about community on three levels[1]—people united by geography (Washington State), attachment (the Communities Connect Network), and common interest (community technology)—a trinity united with the goal of empowering all people through digital inclusion.

March 31, 2008, was a day like no other in Washington State or even across the country for anyone involved in community technology, information and communication technology (ICT), the digital divide, the information have and have-nots, digital inclusion, digital inequality, information poverty, or public access computing. It marked a watershed moment as Washington State joined other states such as California, Illinois, Minnesota, and Ohio[2] that have enacted laws or regulations supporting community technology. As Governor Christine Gregoire signed Senate Bill 6438 (see Appendix A), this ground-breaking law defined community technology in the State of Washington, making community technology programs eligible for state funding and providing recognition of the contributions they have made over the years to the individuals, families, and communities they serve. The bill also provided $500,000 in state funds to assist community technology organizations in Washington in achieving their missions over the following year.

The quest to bring legal definition to community technology in Washington State is the story of promoting digital inclusion and has far-reaching implications because it is about communicating impact. In the U.S., one can argue that it began in the mid-1980s when academics and civilians started using the internet—or USENET (Unix Users Network), more specifically—changing what primarily had been the domain of the U.S. military, developed as ARPANET in the 1960s (Zakon, 2008). As Baron (2008, p. 13) explains, "Homegrown bulletin board systems (BBSs), carried over telephone dial-up lines, connected clusters of friends and helped create the earliest online social communities. While the best known of these groups was the WELL (Whole Earth 'Lectronic Link), the number of online communities quickly mushroomed." A burgeoning example of attempts to promote community inclusion in the 1990s were Free-Nets, "online community networks that provided the public with one-stop shopping using community-oriented discussions, question-and-answer forums, access to governmental and social services, along with local information, email, and internet access" (Pettigrew, Durrance, & Unruh, 2002, p. 895; see also Schuler, 1994, 1996). As the World Wide Web was introduced in the early 1990s and the millennium approached, heralding a rapidly evolving sophistication in how people communicated in synchronous and asynchronous modes, grassroots organizations, academics, funders, and government together began asking, "How can we ensure that all people have equal opportunity to learn, access, use, and benefit from technology in their daily lives?"

Early conversations regarding access focused on the "digital divide," and as one might expect in retrospect, on telecommunications, connectivity, dial-up, and policy issues largely regarding poverty during the late 1980s. The term "digital divide," which focused on the "haves" and "have-nots," was popularized by the "Falling through the Net" report (1995), sponsored by the U.S. National Telecommunications and Information Administration (NTIA), by Servon (2002) and international comparisons by Norris (2001), Orbicom (2003), and others. However, despite its widespread usage, the term "digital divide" is problematic for several reasons as Warschauer (2003, pp. 6–7) explains. First, "a digital divide is marked not only by physical access to computers and connectivity but also by access to the additional resources that allow people to use technology well." As Warschauer argues, the importance of physical availability and connectivity overshadows the roles of content, language, education, literacy, community, and social resources in community technology use.[3] Second, Warschauer faulted the bipolar assumption that society can be easily divided into those who have access to technology and those who do not; instead, he argued, like others of the day, that gradations or degrees of access exist, a point especially significant when considering race and income. Third, the digital divide label implies a chain of causality, that because one is poor economically, then one also has poor technology access, and vice versa. As a research concept, "digital divide" is thus hard to isolate, study, and make statistical inferences from. Fourth, as a guide for practice, digital divide overemphasizes technological solutions, not leaving space for other ways in which people come together around and benefit from community technology.

For many advocates, a more positive term for the new millennium is "digital inclusion" because it puts people first.[4,5,6] The definition of digital inclusion used throughout this book, which borrows from the "Falling through the Net" NTIA report (2000) and others, is the cornerstone of the Communities Connect Network's philosophy. Encompassing three areas: 1) access, 2) technology literacy, and 3) relevant online content and services, digital inclusion seeks equity for all residents, as well as small businesses and community-based (nonprofit) organizations. The three areas include the following components:

1. Access
    a. Connectivity to the internet
    b. End user equipment (hardware and software, including tools for people with disabilities)
2. Technology literacy
    a. Skills required to utilize the equipment and internet effectively for essential services, education, employment, civic engagement, and cultural participation
3. Relevant online content and services
    a. Services available for those in need
    b. Culturally and educationally appropriate design
    c. Marketing and placement appropriate to reach underserved communities
    d. Enabling content production and distribution by lower capacity residents, businesses, and organizations

This three-prong definition of digital inclusion means that communities, including government, have to provide more than simple computer ownership. The Communities Connect Network believes this philosophy enables it to be more strategic about research, investments, and program delivery.

A strong definition of digital inclusion lays the foundation for describing community technology itself, the subject of this book. As now stated in Washington State law, a community technology program means:

> A program, including a digital inclusion program, engaged in diffusing information and communications technology in local communities, particularly in underserved areas. These programs may include, but are not limited to, programs that provide education and skill-building opportunities, hardware and software, internet connectivity, and development of locally relevant content and delivery of vital services through technology. (Washington State Law E2SSB 6438.SL, Section 7, Paragraph 2, lines 18-25)

For more than two decades now, all types of community gathering places—from dedicated community technology centers to youth and community centers to schools, libraries, and 4-H clubs to seniors' associations, low-income housing, churches, radio stations, and municipal offices—have been involved in providing community technology programming in towns and cities across the U.S. Other pertinent facts about community technology programs include the following:

- "They are delivered onsite and online—many service organizations have installed computer labs for learning (also called community technology centers, CTCs, or telecentres). Some nonprofits have been created specifically to provide multimedia, media literacy, and technology educations programs, but for most organizations, the technology tools are used to further a larger mission.
- They increase residents' self-sufficiency and capacity to learn, develop their skills and talents, and help people more fully participate in community and civic affairs. The result is a more educated community, more able workforce, new entrepreneurs, safer kids, and a better connected community. Community technology programs also

help develop consumers of information technology products and services.

- They are often supported by a patchwork of resources and undercapitalized. Organizations running community technology programs are very successful at leveraging and extending the resources they have but are challenged in finding sustainable funding sources. Organizations often secure funds through a combination of fundraising events, donations of products and services, volunteer labor, specific program grants, and some revenue generated programs. The mix varies considerably depending upon the capacity and nature of the organization, setting, and services provided.
- They need to be separate—the application of information and communications technology to education, human services, workforce training, civic engagement, and community development is a rapidly evolving field. Just as in the development of technology for the business sector, this takes training, strategic planning, and strategic investment. Community technology programs must be integrated into regular programs and service delivery, but this requires the development and sustainability of specific expertise, program content and infrastructure." (communities connect.wikispaces.com/CT+ Definitions)

To varying degrees, the collective efforts of CTCs have resulted in regional and statewide associations, and a national association, the Community Technology Centers' Network (CTCNet; 2008), as well as academic programs/curricula and research centers at universities across the U.S. and worldwide (e.g., Information and Society Center of the University of Washington Information School, 2009; Community Informatics Initiative, University of Illinois at Urbana-Champaign, 2008; Gurstein, 2007). But whether one refers to the field as community technology, community informatics, or information and communication technology, seminal questions remain of how to identify the impacts of community technology programs and how to successfully communicate those impacts in ways that are heard by policymakers and other key stakeholders. What counts as community technology use? Getting a job or a better score on a test is pretty straight forward, but what if someone uses a CTC on someone else's behalf? Is that still considered a form of use? What about the indirect ways in which people benefit from CTC use, such as feeling more connected to society or just feeling happier? How can that be measured? Through identifying and communicating such complex forms of impacts, CTCs can attain long-term sustainability and achieve digital inclusion.

This book is about the impacts of community technology on the people of Washington State, as learned and told by the Communities Connect Network in its mission to achieve digital inclusion for all. In the following chapters, the Communities Connect Network story of identifying and communicating impact is presented in parts: the methodology (Chapter 3); seven case studies from across the State and an analysis of their impact (Chapters 4 through 11); our high level framework for measuring impact (the Situated Logic Model) and ideas for using it in the real world (Chapters 12 through 14); and a list of resources for professionals and academics interested in learning more about community technology and digital inclusion (Chapter 15). We begin Chapter 2 with an overview of the Communities Connect Network.

Endnotes

1. While "community" is undoubtedly one of the most bandied about terms in the academy, Willmott's (1986) tripartite distinction is one of the clearest and most useful.
2. In California, Senate Bill 1863 in 2002 (info.sen.ca.gov/pub/01-02/bill/sen/sb_1851-1900/sb_1863_bill_20020828_chaptered.pdf) and Bill 720 in 2003 (info.sen.ca.gov/pub/03-04/bill/sen/sb_0701-0750/sb_720_bill_20030925_chaptered.pdf) determined that the Public Utilities Commission must provide a nonprofit community technology program to address inequality of access to advanced telecommunications services. Three million dollars was allocated to assist qualifying organizations in this effort. The influential Illinois "Eliminate the Digital Divide Law" passed in 2000 that "establish[ed] educational and economic development initiatives that will bridge the digital divide, making possible a society in which all individuals can benefit from the opportunities provided by the new technologies" focused on community technology centers and other community-based organizations (tinyurl.com/5p4 ncu). This law was amended in 2007 to increase the size of grants that institutions can receive and created a working group to review grant applications and find financial support for the program, which had not been provided by the legislature (www.iasb.com/law/digest07.cfm and www.ilctc.org). Ohio

(www.clevelanddigitalvision.org/exec_order_broadband_ohio.doc) and Minnesota (www.revisor.leg.state.mn.us/statutes/?id=16E&view=chapter&year=1998#stat.16E.13) have also addressed community technology through executive orders and statutes.

3. Warschauer uses the popular term "ICT" (information and communication technology).
4. In this regard, authors such as Warschauer (2003, p. 8) prefer the broader term "social inclusion," a European perspective that "refer(s) to the extent that individuals, families, and communities are able to fully participate in society and control their own destinies, taking into account a variety of factors related to economic resources, employment, health, education, housing, recreation, culture, and civic engagement."
5. DiMaggio and Hargittai (2004), frequent authors on digital inclusion, have also popularized "digital inequality."
6. Despite the widely accepted change in nomenclature by academics, the term "digital divide" has not died out completely. A 2005 review by Dewan and Riggins is worth noting.

References

S.B. 720, 2003 Leg., (Cal. 2003)

S.B. 1863, 2002 Leg., (Cal. 2002)

S.B. 6438, 60th Leg., 2008 Reg. Sess. (Wash. 2008)

H.B. 3650, 94th Leg. 2006 Reg. Sess. (Ill. 2006)

30 Ill. Comp. Stat. 780 (2000)

Minn. Stat. 16E.13 (1998)

Exec. Order No. 24S (Ohio 2007)

Baron, N. S. (2008). *Always on: Language in an online and mobile world.* Oxford: Oxford University Press.

Communities Connect. (2009). Wikispaces.com/CT+Definitions

Community Informatics Initiative, University of Illinois at Urbana-Champaign. (2008). ilabs.inquiry.uiuc.edu/ilab/cii

Community Technology Centers' Network (CTCNet). (2008). ctcnet.org

Dewan, S., & Riggins, F. J. (2005). The digital divide: Current and future research directions. *Journal of the Association for Information Systems, 6*(12), 298–337.

DiMaggio, P., Hargittai, E., Celeste, C., & Shafer, S. (2004). Digital inequality: From unequal access to differentiated use. In K. Neckman (Ed.), *Social Inequality* (pp. 355–400). New York: Russell Sage Foundation.

Gurstein, M. (2007). What is community informatics? (And why does it matter?). Milan: Polimetrica. eprints.rclis.org/12372 ref from p. 9

Information and Society Center of the University of Washington Information School. (2008). isc.washington.edu

National Telecommunications and Information Administration (NTIA). (1995). Falling through the Net: A survey of the "have nots" in rural and urban America. Washington, DC. www.ntia.doc.gov/ntiahome/falling thru.html

National Telecommunications and Information Administration (NTIA). (2000). Falling through the Net: Toward digital inclusion. Washington, DC. www.ntia.doc.gov/ntiahome/fttn00/contents00.html

Norris, P. (2001). *Digital divide: Civic engagement, information poverty, and the internet worldwide.* Cambridge: Cambridge University Press.

Orbicom. (2003). *Monitoring the digital divide ... and beyond.* Orbicom, Canadian Agency for International Development, InfoDev and UNESCO, 161 pp. www.infodev.org/files/836_file_The_Digital_Divide.pdf

Pettigrew, K. E., Durrance, J. C., & Unruh, K. T. (2002). Facilitating community information-seeking using the internet: Findings from three public library-community network systems. *Journal of the American Society for Information Science & Technology, 53*(11), 894–903.

Schuler, D. (1994). Community networks: Building a new participatory medium. *Communications of the ACM, 37,* 39–51.

Schuler, D. (1996). *New community networks: Wired for change.* New York: Addison-Wesley.

Servon, L. J. (2002). *Bridging the digital divide: Technology, community, and public policy.* Malden, MA: Blackwell.

Warschauer, M. (2003). *Technology and social inclusion: Rethinking the digital divide.* Cambridge: MIT Press.

Willmott, P. (1986). *Social networks: Informal care and public policy.* London: Policy Studies Institute.

Zakon, R. H. (2008). Hobbes' Internet Timeline v8.2. Zakon Group LLC. OpenConf. www.zakon.org/robert/internet/timeline.

CHAPTER 2

The Communities Connect Network

Michael Crandall and Karen E. Fisher

The Communities Connect Network (CCN; www.communitiesconnect.org) grew out of a long-standing program funded by the Bill & Melinda Gates Foundation as one of its earliest philanthropic efforts, the Community Access to Technology program (MGS Consulting Services, 2008). Begun in 1999, the program provided funding for community organizations using technology to assist their users in improving their lives, increasing their knowledge, and meeting basic needs. In 2005, the foundation made the first steps toward moving the program into the community it served through an award to Washington State University's Center to Bridge the Digital Divide (Fleenor & Palmer, 2005). It intended to build capacity within community technology organizations across the state. The center administered a grant program, organized a statewide forum to bring members of community technology groups together for the first time (October 2005), and began to map out a strategy for strengthening the voice and presence of community technology organizations in the state.

As part of that early effort, a statewide steering committee was formed to map out a strategic vision for community technology in the coming years. The core of that vision was a self-organized, self-sustaining network of those who were interested in and passionate about community technology efforts in Washington State. The group was named the Communities Connect Network. A proposal was put forward to the Bill & Melinda Gates Foundation that provided the underpinnings for a two-year effort to organize and develop this network, and funding was provided to a consortium of five groups led by Washington State University's Center to Bridge the Digital Divide (www.cbdd.wsu.edu) to make this possible: the City of Seattle's Community Technology Program (www.seattle.gov/tech), Stone Soup (www.nwstonesoup.org), One Economy (www.one-economy.com), NPower Seattle (www.npowerseattle.org), and the University of Washington's Information School (www.ischool.washington.edu).

Each of the five organizations had specific individual objectives as part of its commitment, but there was also a shared commitment of working together on a larger strategy: to combine the efforts of each group toward a common goal of building a sustainable organization that would carry the mission of the initiative forward in the future (see Figure 2.1 for a map of project objectives). Over the two years of the grant, the partners were able to grow a statewide network of community technology programs, conduct substantial research on the activities and impacts of those programs, train and educate staff from more than 80 community technology programs in outreach and evaluation activities, and build an interactive online and face-to-face network of community technology providers throughout the state.

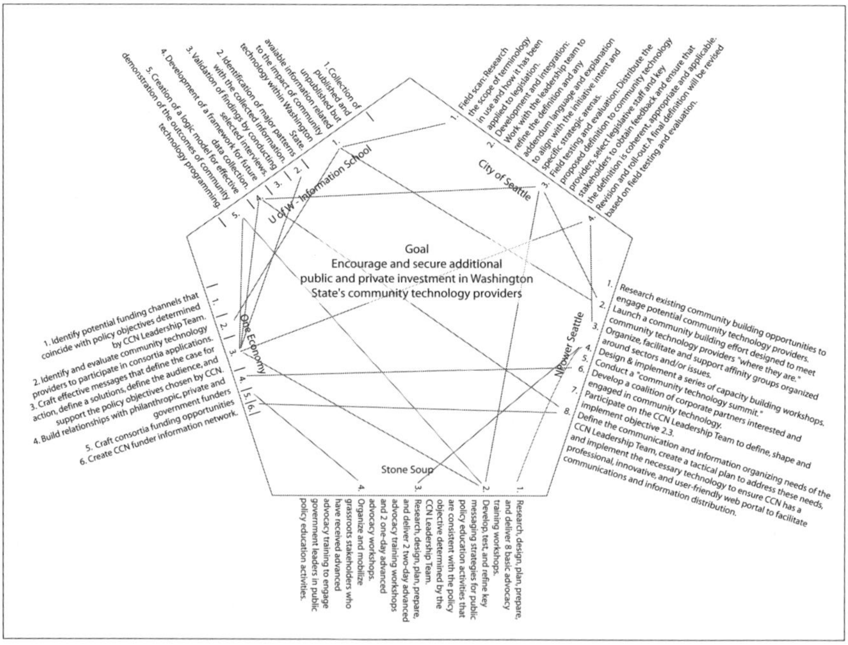

Figure 2.1 Map of CCN Project Objectives (created by Matthew Mitchell of Washington State University's Center to Bridge the Digital Divide)

In 2007, early steps were taken to engage the legislature in discussions about the work of CCN through meetings with key individuals who had interest in the work that CCN and its members were doing. In November 2007, a concentrated effort was made to engage the Washington State Legislature in this activity by taking the results of the research study and the voices of the providers directly to the Senate and House through participation in a series of hearings in the state capital (Crandall, 2007; see Appendix B). The hearings were also used as a way to provide training in outreach and communication to the providers by linking the testimony to a pre-hearing workshop sponsored by the CCN where all parties involved practiced presentations and worked on a coordinated message.

Following the hearings, a series of open houses was sponsored by individual community technology groups in their local communities, with key legislators specifically invited, along with others in the community. These open houses were facilitated by CCN with resources and training provided in advance to ensure successful messaging and engagement (communitiesconnect.wikispaces.com/Hosting+an+Open+House+workspace). At the same time, CCN partners were engaging directly with interested legislators to provide additional information and suggestions on how they could effectively address the issues raised in the hearings in a way that would provide support across the state for community technology organizations. A poster describing the results of CCN's efforts was also presented to the legislators and their staff at the annual higher education legislative days in the capital to keep the efforts visible as the legislative session progressed (see Figure 2.2).

As a result of the hearings, the open houses, and the individual discussions with legislators, two bills designed to codify recognition of community technology programs as legal entities were created by a broad coalition of interested representatives and senators. These were introduced separately in the short session at the beginning of 2008 and, through a rather tortuous process of compromise, change, and adaptation (with strong support from key legislators who had worked closely with CCN), made it through the legislative process in a remarkably short time, resulting in the Second Substitute Senate Bill 6438 (see Appendix A), signed into law by Governor Christine Gregoire on March 31, 2008 (see the timeline of CCN activity in Figure 2.3).

As stated in Chapter 1, not only did the bill define community technology in a way that incorporates the key essence of digital inclusion by making sure that the services and content being offered by

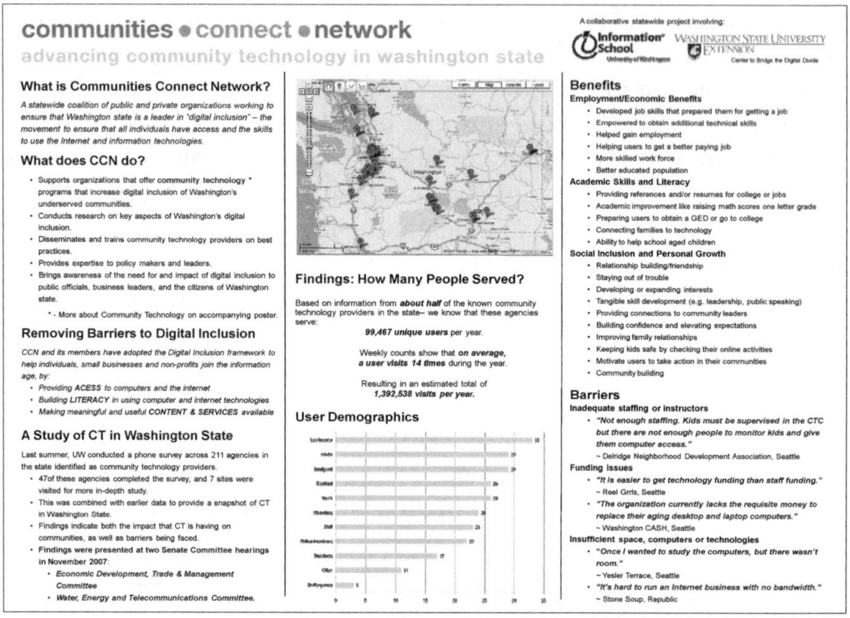

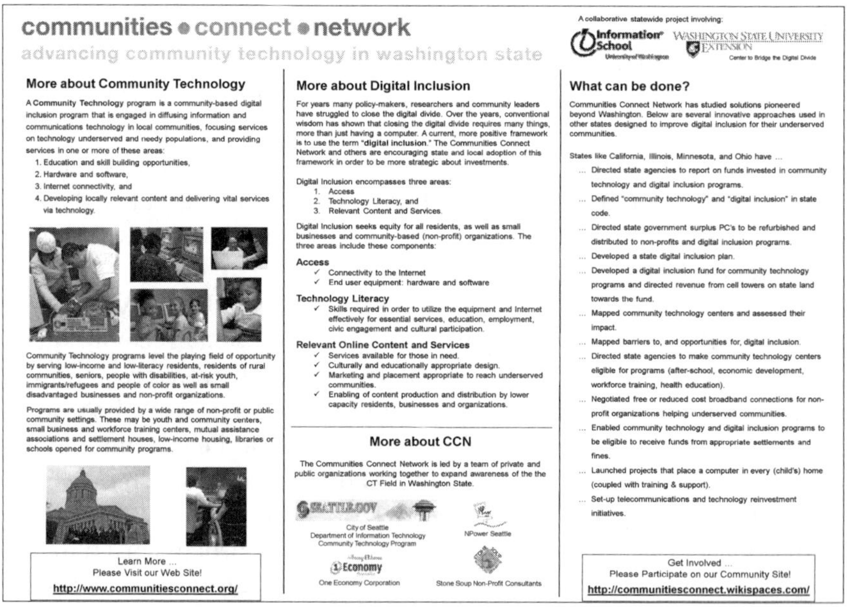

Figure 2.2 Washington State Higher Education Legislative Day Poster (Crandall & Mitchell, 2008)

- **1999**– Community Access to Technology program starts at Bill & Melinda Gates Foundation
- **April 2005**– Communities Connect grant and capacity building program established at Washington State University through funding from Bill & Melinda Gates Foundation
- **October 2005**– First statewide gathering of CTC providers at Big Tent Meeting
- **June 2006**– Communities Connect Network (CCN) consortium formed with funding from Bill & Melinda Gates Foundation to build grassroots organization
- **August 2006**– CCN statewide kickoff meeting
- **September 2006**– University of Washington (UW) Information School commences field research
- **January 2007**– UW Information School presents preliminary results to legislature at Higher Education Day
- **December 2007**– CCN presentations to legislative committees
- **January 2008**– UW presents research results to legislature at Higher Education Day
- **January 2008**– SSB6438 passes legislature
- **March 2008**– SSB6438 signed into law by Governor Christine Gregoire, establishing definition of community technology in Washington & allocating $500,000 for capacity building and grants under the Community Technology Opportunity Program (CTOP)
- **June 2008**– CCN becomes an independent organization under fiscal sponsorship of Puget Sound Center for Teaching, Learning and Technology (PSCTLT)
- **June 2008**– CTOP program awards $350,000 in grants to CTC providers
- **December 2008**– Second statewide Legislative Day sponsored by CCN

Figure 2.3 CCN Timeline

the providers is of equal importance to the technology itself, but it also allocated $500,000 in the upcoming budget year to provide assistance to community technology organizations in achieving their objectives through a state-funded grant program. That program is now underway as the Community Technology Opportunity Program (www.cbdd.wsu.edu/ctop), and grants to 10 organizations have been awarded for the coming year. The research framework presented in Part III was developed and refined as part of the CCN efforts over the preceding two years and is being used to evaluate the impact these grants will have on the individuals, families, and communities associated with the projects. The results will be used to further the advocacy efforts of CCN in the future.

CCN itself has evolved into a self-sustaining organization under the fiscal sponsorship of the Puget Sound Center for Teaching, Learning and Technology, with an independent director, board, and advisory council. It is continuing the organizational, training, advocacy, and outreach work begun in 2006. The advisory council, named the Council on Digital Inclusion, is composed of representatives from industry, associations and unions, government, education, and community technology practitioners, and extends the network deeper into the policy arena. The next few years will provide CCN with ample opportunities to bring the work that community technology organizations do into multiple venues and to continue to provide visibility and develop support for their mission.

References

S.B. 6438, 60th Leg., 2008 Reg. Sess. (Wash. 2008)

Communities Connect. (2008). Hosting an open house workspace. Communities Connect Network wiki. communitiesconnect.wikispaces.com/Hosting+an+Open+House+workspace

Crandall, M. (2007). Digital inclusion in action: How Washington's community technology nonprofits provide access, literacy and content. Presentation to Washington Senate Economic Development, Trade and Management Committee. Olympia, WA.

Crandall, M., & Mitchell, M. (2008). Communities connect network. *Washington Higher Education Legislative Day*. Olympia, WA.

Fleenor, D., & Palmer, K. (2005). "WSU to Administer Gates Foundation's Community Access to Technology Program." Bill & Melinda Gates Foundation, Seattle, WA. April 6, 2005. www.gatesfoundation.org/press-releases/Pages/wsu-community-access-to-technology-050406.aspx

MGS Consulting Services. (2008). "Community Access to Technology Program Evaluation Report—Year 3." Seattle, WA. www.mgs-us.com/Our Clients/CAT_Final_Eval.pdf

CHAPTER 3

The Research Context

Michael Crandall and Karen E. Fisher

As discussed in Chapter 2, a key activity that Communities Connect Network (CCN) focused on before, during, and after the legislative session was educating stakeholders on how community technology organizations were making a difference in the state regarding digital inclusion. The remainder of this book focuses on one particular aspect of the CCN effort—the research describing and communicating the impact of the community technology programs in Washington State on the individuals, families, and communities they serve.

Understanding the Landscape

To better understand how community technology organizations promote digital inclusion in Washington State, several research methods were employed. We began by conducting a systematic review of the policy, research, and technical literature pertaining to community technology, digital inclusion, and other related subjects to see how others had framed the impact of community technology. Finding little in the literature to inform our investigation, we built upon the evaluation research of the Washington Information Network (WIN) 2-1-1 Telephone Information and Referral Service, which involved deriving a logic model for describing impact to different stakeholder groups (Saxton, Naumer, & Fisher, 2007). That model provided the impetus for the more sophisticated Situated Logic Model described in Chapter 12 of this book.

Following extensive empirical research of the community technology scene across Washington State together with further conceptual analysis within the policy arena, the Situated Logic Model describes the work of community technology centers (CTCs) as creating the capacity for other programs to deliver services. The model thus examines the work of CTCs as building capacity within the social service infrastructure, demonstrating the relationships between program logic models and the capacity-building role of CTCs at a systematic level.

The other primary methods used in this study were a telephone survey of community technology providers and case studies comprising interviews, focus groups, and field observation with users and staff at seven organizations. A map of the CTCs that participated in the phone survey and field site visits can be seen in Figure 3.1 (Crandall, 2007).

As shown in Table 3.1 (Naumer & Fisher, 2007), any single research method has its limitations; therefore, researchers often use mixed methods (quantitative and qualitative approaches together) to yield the strongest research design. To train our case study team, comprised of students in the master's of Library and Information Science program at the University of Washington Information School, we used the Outcomes Toolkit by Durrance and Fisher (2005). Published

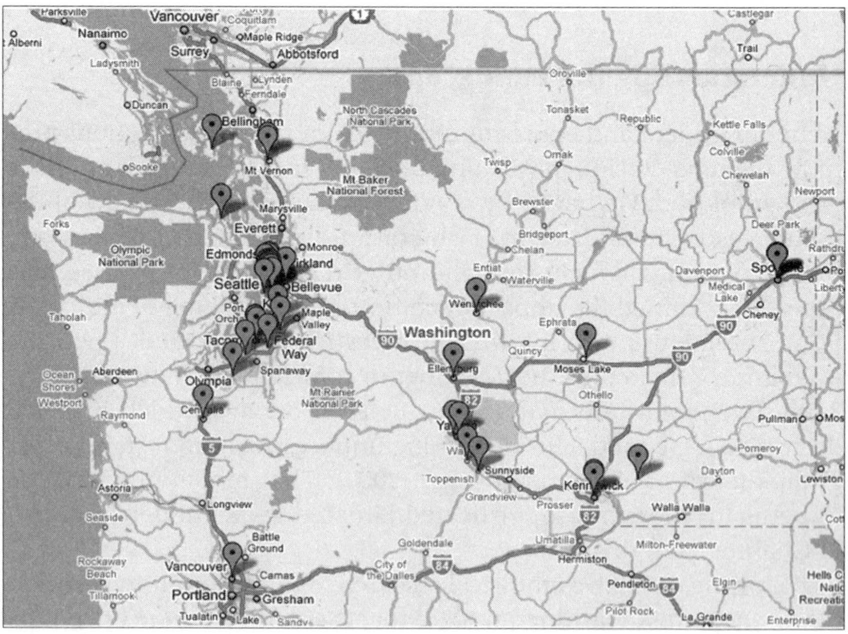

Figure 3.1 Map of Survey and Site Visit Community Technology Centers

online and as a monograph, *How Libraries and Librarians Help: A Guide to Identifying User-Centered Outcomes*, this toolkit is a four-step, context-based approach aimed at helping community-based organizations understand the impact of their information services. Durrance and Fisher developed the toolkit by working with community librarians around the country, and they explain how to work with limited resources while optimizing results, emphasizing how statistics plus stories are the most effective means to communicate impact to policymakers and other stakeholders.

Table 3.1 Data Collection Methods—Advantages and Disadvantages

Method	Advantages	Disadvantages
Observation	Allows for a variety of perspectives May be unobtrusive, reducing observer effect Actions may be observed instead of relying on description Allows for studying behavior that might not lend itself to description Permits for studying people who may not be willing to participate otherwise	Subjects may change behavior when they know they are being observed (observer effect) Requires access to observe spontaneous event or behavior Not all types of activity lend themselves to observation Can be very time consuming Is dependent subject to the observer's interpretation of events
Interview	Immediacy—data may be quickly collected May allow for mutual exploration of ideas between interviewer and subject May allow for the investigation of causation Provides an opportunity for personal contact with subjects and increased awareness of phenomena being studied	May be time consuming When subjects are being compensated, could be costly May not be critical and hence prone to interviewer bias
Diaries	Lends itself to studying behavior over time rather than a point in time Allows participants to be active in data collection Allows for participants to determine what is important	May result in unstructured data May be costly if participants are paid Diaries may be inconsistent Requires participants to be self-disciplined May be prone to participant bias; subjects may change behavior or report different aspects of their behavior in their diaries
Surveys	Allows for a relatively large sampling May allow data to be collected for hard-to-access populations using mail or internet May be a fast way to collect data Provides for structured data	Ability to explore open-ended questions may be limited by survey instrument length and subjects' ability to articulate responses in writing May be prone to bias by subjects inaccurately reporting their actions or behavior May be costly when participants are paid, or response rates could be low when not adequately compensated Could be subject to sampling error according to which subjects respond to the survey

Think Aloud	May provide a unique opportunity to better understand cognitive tasks that are difficult to uncover using other approaches May provide an opportunity to more deeply explore thought processes for certain behaviors May provide a unique way to understand the context of actions	May be time consuming May be costly when participants are paid Requires participants to adequately describe behavior May be prone to observer effect, or process of thinking out loud may artificially alter actions and behaviors
Focus Groups	Allows for open exploration of ideas Group dynamic may provide for the development of questions not considered by researcher May result in rich detail and explanation of an issue or behavior as a result of multiple perspectives being offered	May be subject to bias toward a dominant participant or participants Subjects may not express themselves as freely in a group as individually Data may be unstructured and may not be focused on phenomena being studied
Text Analysis	May be unobtrusive, reducing observer effect Allows for a variety of perspectives in examining data Actions may be observed instead of relying on description Allows for studying behavior that might not lend itself to description Permits for studying people who may not be willing to participate otherwise	Subjects may change behavior when they know they are being observed (observer effect) Not all types of activity lend themselves to observation using personal documents Can be very time consuming May result in a lot of extraneous data Is subject to the observer's interpretation of text May lack context that lends itself to interpreting the artifact (such as a conversation preceding the sending of an email)
Case Study	Provides for the identification of themes, characteristics, and conditions Allows for a broad holistic examination of a situation May help to identify what works and what does not work May provide a contextual understanding that could inform additional research methods	Subject to bias from case study writer Requires access to phenomena being described and often dependent on third parties for descriptions of events or actions Limited to one particular moment in time or one situation

Surveying the CTCs

For the CCN study, Stage One comprised a telephone survey to gather information about the number of users and uses, the type of services being offered, and other characteristics. From an initial list of more than 200 potential agencies identified from existing directories of CTCs and programs, staff from 47 agencies responded to the survey. A full transcript of the survey questions can be found in Appendix C. Additional information providing only the number of users for another 59 organizations was obtained from grant records at the Bill & Melinda Gates Foundation.

The survey results provided insights into the nature of the centers offering community technology programs across the state. Three-quarters of the programs had been in existence for more than five years, indicating both the community need and the success that most of the programs had in meeting that need for an extended period of time. Slightly less than two-thirds of the centers (64 percent) had less than five staff members, with another 19 percent having between five and 10 people on staff. The small size of most of these centers reflects the budgetary constraints and localized nature of their services. Almost all of the centers are nonprofits that self-identify as neighborhood community or service centers of some type.

Using the combined results from the survey and previous information from grantees in the Bill & Melinda Gates Foundation's Community Access to Technology program (equal to about half of the known community technology providers in the state), we know that these agencies serve a minimum of *99,467 unique users per year*. Weekly counts show that on average, a user visits 14 times during the year, resulting in an estimated total of 1,392,538 visits per year. These numbers are based upon the most conservative estimates from the original data and can be considered the absolute minimum for the populations being served. If the remaining organizations that did not respond to the survey provide equivalent services, these numbers would almost double. This is a large number of people for a state with a population of 6,395,798; clearly, community technology is providing a much-needed service not being met by other organizations in the state.

The types of audiences being served by the organizations are also significant in understanding the full picture of how these organizations fit into their communities. The findings of the telephone survey, as shown in Figure 3.2, indicate that youth, immigrants, and members of low-income households were frequent users of those centers.

It is evident that these programs are reaching some of the most underserved segments of their communities and providing them with services from which they might otherwise be excluded. This is further reinforced by the top two reasons these people are using the services of the community technology organizations, according to the staff who responded to the survey (see Figure 3.3). Doing better at school, connecting with other people and community services, and learning new skills, such as technology, job, and independence skills, were all highlighted as important reasons users visit CTCs.

Another set of findings from the survey centered on the barriers staff found to accomplishing their objectives, as shown in Table 3.2. Not surprisingly, funding was the top issue identified, but there were a number of other impediments that were called out relating to resource availability, facilities to help users with childcare,

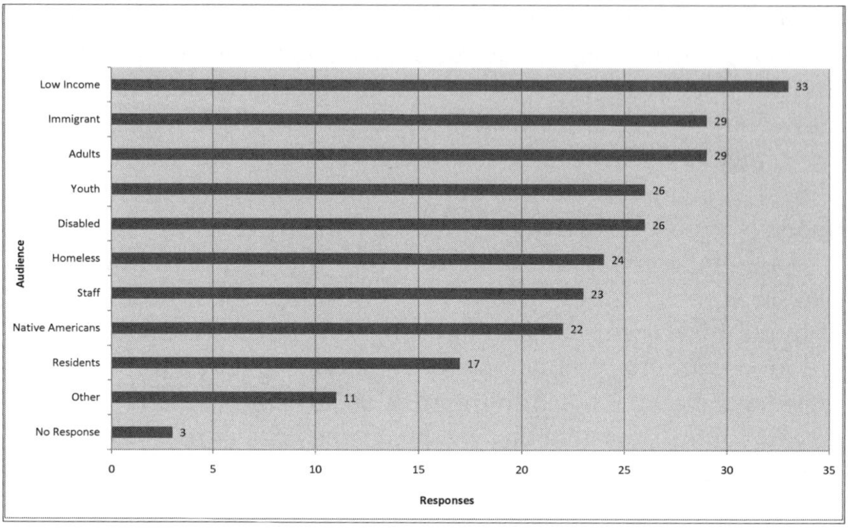

Figure 3.2 Populations Served by 47 CTCs in Washington State (more than one response possible for each agency; total exceeds number of organizations surveyed)

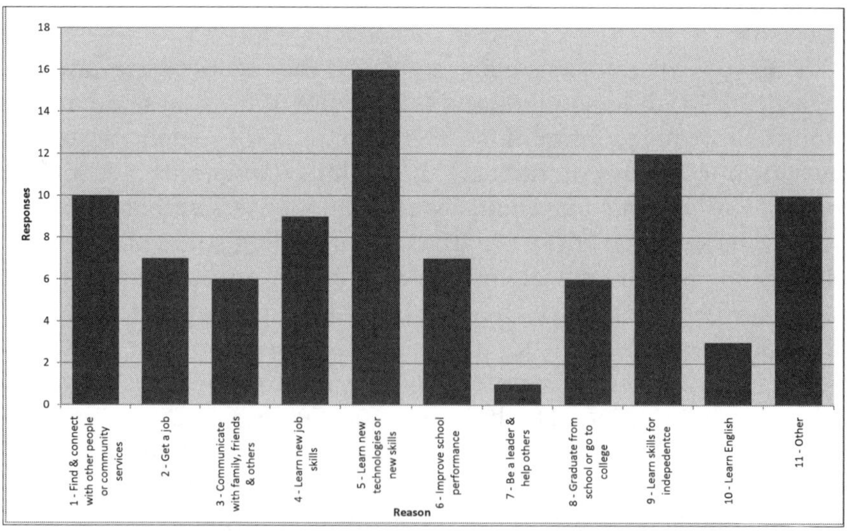

Figure 3.3 Top Two Reasons People Use Washington CTCs (more than one response possible for each agency; total exceeds number of organizations surveyed)

Table 3.2 Barriers to Success in CTCs Identified by Staff

Phone Survey	Staff
No barriers	50%
Funding	40%
Childcare	22%
Limited resources	17%
Capacity	15%
Training	5%
Transportation/location	18%
Limited hours	8%
Staffing	17%
Membership/registration/fee required	8%
Other	60%

transportation, or lack of training in the use of the technology. This area will be discussed in more detail in Chapter 11, with users of CTCs identifying many of the same issues as impeding their CTC activity. It is these barriers that CCN aims to help address through providing a stronger network among the organizations throughout the state, and a more coherent and visible voice at the statewide policy level.

Visiting the CTCs

Stage Two, the case studies, involved interviews and focus groups with staff and users (age 14 and older) along with field observation in seven different CTCs across the state. The field provided a much richer set of contextual information that helped inform the survey results from Stage One. To gain a broader picture of community technology's impact, Stage Two purposefully investigated organizations that targeted such populations as immigrants, youth, and residents of low-income housing centers. Furthermore, the CTCs were selected for their diverse locations such as Seattle and Tacoma (metropolitan areas), Jefferson County (Olympic Peninsula), and Yakima Valley (Eastern Washington). The specific sites included:

- Reel Grrls – Seattle-based CTC that uses technology to empower young women (Chapter 4)
- La Casa Hogar – Eastern Washington CTC that brings families into the community (Chapter 5)
- 4-H Network News – Jefferson County CTC that teaches youth to build community (Chapter 6)
- Tacoma Clubhouse – Pierce County CTC that helps students succeed (Chapter 7)
- Yesler Terrace Community Center – Seattle CTC that helps adults grow out of poverty (Chapter 8)
- Washington CASH – Seattle CTC that assists adults with building financial assets (Chapter 9)
- Delridge Neighborhoods Development Association – Seattle CTC that integrates learning with low-income housing (Chapter 10)

Both the staff and the user interview guides, shown in the sidebars on pages 25 and 26, consisted of primarily open-ended questions that were intended to explore the nature of what it means to provide or participate in using community technology services, respectively. The interviews and focus groups ranged from 20–30 minutes with the staff interviews typically taking longer. In keeping with regulations set by the University of Washington's Internal Review Board for studying human subjects, minors (users between the ages of 14 and 17) were required to participate in focus groups as opposed to one-on-one interviews. Each user received $10 for participating in an interview or focus group. The research team also kept extensive field notes about their observations regarding the CTCs and their stakeholders, and gathered background materials.

Community Technology Center Evaluation Interview Guide for Staff

Note: This generic instrument is for conducting 45-minute interviews with administrators and staff of CTCs in Washington State. Data will be used to identify user outcomes and implementation issues.

Staff Code: CTC Code:
Date: Place of Interview:
Length of Interview:

Questions:

1. How long have you been working with the CTC?
2. What does the CTC provide?
3. Who are its users?
4. What is your role at the CTC? (What are your responsibilities?)
5. How would you characterize the successes of the CTC?
6. How have individual users been helped?
7. Why is your center important to its users?
8. What information do users seek most often?
9. How often does your average user visit the center?
10. In what ways have benefits been accrued by users' families? The community at-large? What is your evidence for these observations?
11. Do you work with other organizations in the community? If so, how? How do they benefit from the services you deliver?
12. What factors hindered the development and offerings of the center?
13. What challenges do the users of your center face in using technology?
14. How could the center be improved?
15. How would you like to see the center develop in the future?
16. What is needed to make this happen?
17. Other comments?

Community Technology Center Evaluation Interview Guide for Users

Note: This generic instrument is for conducting 20- to 30-minute interviews with users of CTCs in Washington State. Data will be used to identify users' learning and individual/family outcomes.

User Code: CTC Code:
Date: Place of Interview:
Length of Interview:

Questions:

1. How did you learn about the CTC?
2. When did you start using the CTC?
3. Do you have access to a computer or the internet anywhere else besides the CTC?
4. How much time have you spent at the CTC?
5. What drew you to the CTC? (What did you want to gain? What is the reason you came here?)
6. Which activities/courses have you taken or tried at the CTC?
7. What did you learn/gain because of the CTC? (Ask for each activity the user participated in.)
8. Did anything make it difficult or prevent you from using the CTC?
9. Is there anything you wanted to do at the CTC that you couldn't do (find information, learn a skill, etc.)?
10. Is the CTC an important place for you? If so, what do you like about the activities/CTC?
11. Are other people you meet at the CTC helpful?
12. How could the activities/CTC be made better?
13. How has your family benefited, if at all, from the CTC?
14. Since you started using the CTC, is there anything you can do now or have accomplished that you could not have done before?
15. Will you continue to use the CTC?

16. Have you recommended the CTC to other people? If so, to whom (not asking for personal names here, just relationship types, e.g., friends, family)?

Demographic questions:

17. What is your age?
18. What is your race/ethnicity?
19. Is English your first language?
20. What is your ZIP code?
21. What is the highest level of education you've completed?
22. How many people are in your household?
23. What is the gender and age of each person in your household?
24. What is your occupation?

The data were analyzed iteratively as they were collected by the team through the sharing of their findings in debriefings; these findings contributed to the construction of a final codebook. This codebook was then applied across all of the interview data and field notes. In addition to identifying emergent themes as they arose during the analytic process, the case studies focused on illuminating data pertaining to individual, family, and community benefits. These three-stakeholder categories were identified in the *How Libraries and Librarians Help* (c.f., Durrance & Fisher, 2005) fieldwork and used to construct data collection instruments and codebooks to study how migrant Hispanic farm workers and their families benefit from CTCs (Fisher, Marcoux, Miller, Sanchez, & Cunningham, 2004), as well as to understand the effects of the Washington Information Network (WIN) 2-1-1 Telephone Information and Referral Service (Saxton, Naumer, & Fisher, 2007). We also designed the questions so that we could learn more about the problems encountered with center use and program development. The findings of the case studies were then analyzed according to the following broad outcomes, which were identified from extensive review of the published literature on community technology and public policy indicators being used to measure impact:

- Employment and economic benefits
- Academic skills and literacy
- Social inclusion and personal growth
- Independence
- Access to information and resources
- Communication

Getting to Impact

The community technology landscape is clearly a complicated one. Numerous small, local organizations are serving diverse populations, usually those that are unable to gain access to technology and services that most of us take for granted. The challenge that the research team faced in trying to make sense of the rich stories and statistics that had been gathered from the field was understanding how best to analyze the impacts these organizations have on the individuals, families, and communities they serve, and then how to present that in a way that meant something to the key stakeholders in the legislative process. The next section of the book shares the stories from the seven case studies, along with the analysis of the impacts of those CTCs. Part 2 lays the foundation for the framework, centered around the Situated Logic Model, which is developed in Part 3.

References

Crandall, M. (2007). Digital inclusion in action: How Washington's community technology nonprofits provide access, literacy and content. Presentation to Washington Senate Economic Development, Trade and Management Committee. Olympia, WA.

Durrance, J. C., & Fisher, K. E. (2005). *How libraries and librarians help: A guide to identifying user-centered outcomes.* Chicago: American Library Association. ibec.ischool.washington.edu/toolkit.php

Fisher, K. E., Marcoux, E., Miller, L. S., Sanchez, A., & Cunningham, E. R. (2004). Information behavior of migrant Hispanic farm workers and their families in the Pacific Northwest. *Information Research,* 10(1), paper 199 (paper given at the *Information Seeking in Context (ISIC)* Conference, Dublin, 2004). InformationR.net/ir/10-1/paper199.html

Google Maps. (2007). Map of telephone survey and site visit community technology programs in Washington State, September 10, 2007. Communities Connect Network. maps.google.com/maps/ms?hl=en&ie=UTF8&msa=0&msid=108807764714930984182.000001132627121b93fa4&z=6

Naumer, C. M., & Fisher, K. E. (2007). Field methods for investigating personal information management. In W. Jones & J. Teevan (Eds.), *Personal information management* (pp. 76–88). Seattle: University of Washington Press.

Saxton, M., Naumer, C. M., & Fisher, K. E. (2007). 2-1-1 information services: Outcomes assessment, benefit-cost analysis, and policy issues. *Government Information Quarterly, 24,* 186–215.

Part 2

Real Life Examples—Making an Impact on the Individual, Family, and Community

CHAPTER 4

Reel Grrls—Using Technology to Empower Young Women

Carol F. Landry

A mere 3 percent of Hollywood cinematographers are women, and no woman has ever won an Academy Award for Film Directing. Reel Grrls, a nonprofit youth media agency based in Seattle, Washington, aims to transform statistics like these by empowering young women to "realize their power, talent and influence through media production" (www.reelgrrls.org). The program is designed for girls aged 13 to 19 years, two-thirds of whom identify as low income and many of whom are homeless or living in foster care. After school each day, the teens learn the basics of video, audio, and film production, develop the analytic skills needed to critically evaluate media and master the steps involved in creating a movie. By becoming media literate, it is believed that these girls will be equipped with the necessary tools to become active and influential members of both their local and global societies.

Reel Grrls History and Context

Reel Grrls began as a one-year pilot program in 2001. Within four years, the organization had gained 501(c)(3) nonprofit status and established itself as a model program in the field of youth media. Reel Grrls video productions have been screened at such notable film festivals as the Seattle Lesbian & Gay Film Festival, Sundance Film Festival (Gen-Y Studio), and Hamptons International Film Festival, and they have also earned the Audience Choice Award at both the LocoMotion Youth Film Festival and San Diego Girls Film Festival.

Girls are recruited from a variety of ethnic and socioeconomic groups, with 65 percent self-identifying as low-income. Program fees run from $55 to $475; however, no girl is turned away due to lack of funds, and full scholarships are given when needed.

At the time of this report, Reel Grrls was situated in the historic Odd Fellows Temple building in Seattle's Capitol Hill neighborhood, pictured in Figure 4.1. The building was constructed in 1908 and is home to a variety of nonprofit enterprises. Reel Grrls occupied a small, two-room office on the fourth floor. When necessary, the center rented additional space by the month or by the hour. In general, the space was challenged to contain all of its occupants, equipment, and materials. Due to the sale of the Odd Fellows Building in 2008, Reel Grrls has since relocated to Seattle's Central District, and it is now in a 1,500-square-foot space remodeled to suit both its programming and administrative needs, right next door to Central Cinema, a 125-seat neighborhood film house.

Equipment available for checkout and use includes eight Macintosh laptop computers and nine digital video recorder cameras. The laptops have software applications for editing film and music, such as Final Cut Pro and Soundtrack Pro. Of the nine digital recorders, three are consumer-grade quality, five are prosumer quality (higher grade than consumer), and, for advanced shoots, the

Figure 4.1 Reel Grrls Location—Historic Odd Fellows Building, Seattle, Washington

highest quality camera is used, a Canon XL1. The consumer-grade cameras are employed when editing content on the computer, while the prosumer cameras are used on film shoots. Most cameras are more than two years old. Various other items such as cables, headsets, and microphones complete the Reel Grrls equipment inventory.

Figure 4.2 Reel Grrls Office and User's Work Area

The Visits

Two visits were made to Reel Grrls to find out more about the impact of the organization. A focus group was conducted with nine of the girls ranging in age from 15 to 23 years (average 18 years): seven Reel Grrls users, one intern, and one adult mentor. Participants had been coming to Reel Grrls for one to two-and-a-half years, with the mentor having worked at the center for nine months. Pizza was provided, and each participant received $10 to compensate for her time. The focus group followed a private Reel Grrls activity and was held in a large room owned by another nonprofit.

Staff interviews were also carried out with the founder and executive director of Reel Grrls and the program manager. The executive director had worked at the organization for seven years, while the program manager had been working there for three months. The researchers also observed the Reel Grrls space during this visit.

Reel Grrls and the Girls Who Use It

In order for any community technology center (CTC) to help its targeted demographic, the potential users must first know that it exists. When asked how they had learned of the program, the teens indicated that they had heard of Reel Grrls from a number of different sources. Some learned from teachers who were familiar with the program, while others participated in school events where the executive director or mentors spoke about the organization. Advertisements for Reel Grrls workshops were also seen in the local paper, and one girl heard about the organization when she attended a Reel Grrls film screening at the central Seattle Public Library. The amount of time users spent at the center was difficult to isolate, as visits varied depending on the programming. When a distinct program was running, girls came to the center on average three times per week, whereas if no program was in operation, the average visit was typically once per week. A program was in progress during our visits, wherein groups of three to four girls were working busily together to create promotional videos for other nonprofit organizations.

With a multitude of options vying for young people's attention, researchers wanted to learn what drew teens to Reel Grrls. Responses suggested that interest in film was the main attraction. For 18-year-old Eleanor,[1] it was film scoring. She recognized that when she came to Reel Grrls two years ago, there was "not much call for a 16-year-old to film score, but now I have something to put on my resume." Others wanted to meet people, network, and have access to quality equipment.

Individual Benefits

It was evident that association with Reel Grrls provided both tangible and intangible outcomes to individual users. According to center staff, the girls were embraced in a secure nonjudgmental environment in which they could learn technology. Staff stated that many schools do not offer media programs and explained that in the few schools that do, programs are typically boy-focused and can be

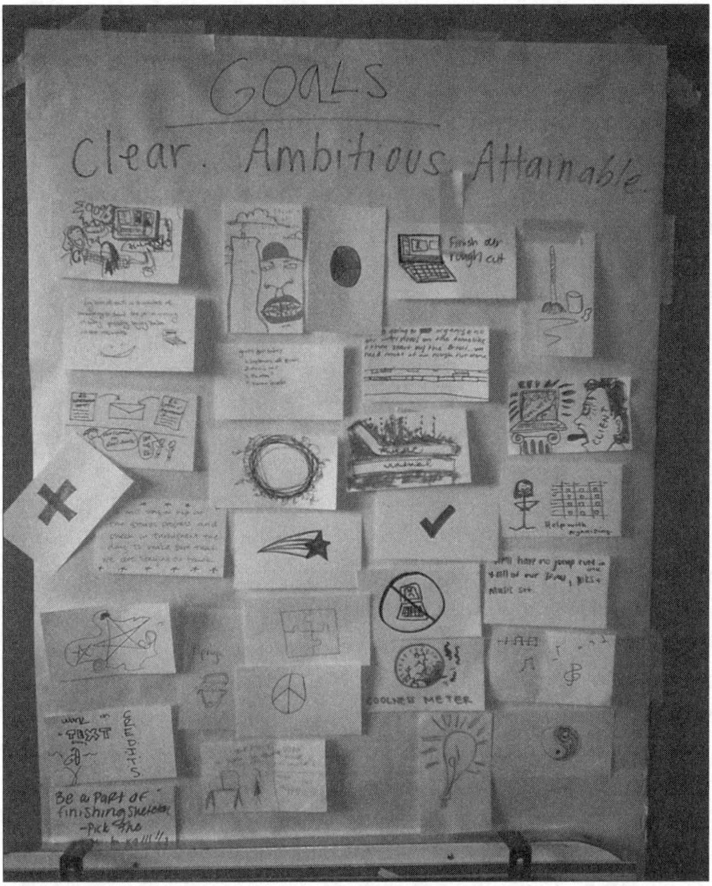

Figure 4.3 List of Reel Grrls Goals for Summer Programs

intimidating to girls. At Reel Grrls, they aim to create a learning ground wherein technology is demystified, while concomitantly providing an open space for teenage girls to meet and work with other girls. Echoing this sentiment, the girls indicated that being a member of an all-female community made them feel safe and valued. According to Tarrah, who had been with the organization for one-and-a-half years, "Learning and making things with girls is good. Other places, guys would try to take control. It's easier not to be in that position." Confirming this view, Brooke, a 19-year-old college sophomore, stated, "It's safe working with girls. I can say anything. At school, you can't say what you like. If you make a mistake, they judge, and you can't work with them positively again." This community spirit built confidence and empowered the girls to take on challenging projects that they may otherwise have avoided.

Reel Grrls places particular emphasis on its mentorship program, whereby positive female role models are brought on board to nurture the girls' professional and personal development. The executive director explained that the mentors support and challenge the girls, much like a sports coach, and that the girls benefit by learning to interface and network with adults. Through these relationships, users connect with other women in the film industry, women who may be able to provide the girls with future training and job opportunities.

It was also revealed that teens learn important life skills such as responsibility, public speaking, interviewing, and team working. Reel Grrls users operate in an atmosphere of trust, where they are made responsible for their actions. The girls are allowed to check out equipment and are trusted to care for that equipment and return it when they are finished using it. Maddie, a 23-year-old mentor, pointed out that when films are screened before large audiences, they are usually followed by a question-and-answer session, which requires the girls to speak publicly about their movies. Users also get experience interviewing people for their documentaries. Eleanor stated that she appreciated learning how to interview and testified that this ability helped her in her activities with Teen Link, an organization that works with teens contemplating suicide. She emphasized, "I have worked at Teen Link for three years now. I can interview better because I try to see from their perspective rather than thinking empathy. It makes the interview better." Learning to work as a team is also an impact of Reel Grrls. In particular, the girls work with others whose lives are dissimilar from their own; for example, prep school users collaborate and learn from homeless users or those living in foster care.

Moreover, girls learned to master high demand, professional skills such as film editing, storyboarding, film production, film scoring, distribution, and communication, all of which can easily transfer to higher education and future employment competencies. This training is all the more significant since many Reel Grrls users are from low-income backgrounds. The program manager spoke of how one homeless girl had made a video about the experience of being homeless and won the "Media That Matters" film festival award. Reel Grrls builds positive self-esteem in its users and fosters a desire to achieve through education and employment. Center staff spoke of how the girls have changed right before their eyes; their confidence grows as they find their voice and learn that people want to listen to what they have to say. With substantial resumes demonstrating significant skills and accomplishments and letters of recommendations from Reel Grrls staff, girls feel equipped to compete with others within and out of the field of media.

Family Benefits

Families also encountered positive outcomes engendered by Reel Grrls activities. Girls reported that they often pass along their technology and media skills to parents or younger siblings so that they, too, may share their stories with others. Parents benefit from Reel Grrls in that they are given assistance with their child's upbringing and professional development. A sense of pride is also fostered among parents as they revel in their children's accomplishments.

Families have been brought closer together because Reel Grrls' users have voiced their concerns and struggles through their movies. One of the girls, Amber, made a film about addiction in her family. Although the topic was difficult due to its emotional content, she noted that "When I was behind the lens, my family talked to me honestly as an adult," something that did not seem to happen otherwise in this 19-year-old's life. The program manager spoke of how one family was even reunited through a Reel Grrls movie. "One girl's mother died when she was young. Her dad was in and out of jail. She did this documentary about her and her dad's relationship. It made an impact on him. Now, she has a relationship with her dad and it came out of her Reel Grrls experience."

Community Benefits

Community outcomes were similarly evident from teenagers' interactions with Reel Grrls. The executive director stated that by hearing what girls have to say, the community-at-large can benefit. To demonstrate this point, the program manager provided the following examples:

> A girl was born to addictive parents. She is a twin and both girls have cerebral palsy. She told her story [through film] and was able to create a discussion guide that is now given out to Al-Anon and Alateen.

> One girl directed a health and safety video for the Ballard School District. It was cool, kid-friendly, and engaging. It communicates an important message that these youth can only tell. Adults can't do that.

Learning to work as a team with members of different ethnic and socioeconomic backgrounds can also have community benefits. As the girls progress to college and work environments, they will have learned valuable skills about cultural inclusion.

In addition, providing a safe and healthy environment for teenagers to participate in can be interpreted as having community benefits. Reel Grrls helps to keep at-risk, homeless, foster care, low-income, and middle-income youth off the streets and out of trouble. It engages teen girls in productive and worthwhile activities, while helping to keep people and communities safe.

Challenges Facing Reel Grrls

Like many nonprofits, Reel Grrls is faced with an assortment of challenges. When asked about difficulties, the Reel Grrls founder and executive director indicated that although funding was the easy answer, the reality is that lack of space and too few staff were the predominant problems. She felt that this hindered recruitment, as girls "had so many choices for after school programs ... like sports." Cramped facilities made it difficult to compete with more alluring options. The executive director also spoke about staffing shortages, stating, "We have a huge program and only four staff. We'd like to reach 200 girls per year. Now it is only 100 per year. We have a large equipment budget, but I would like to allocate it for staff."

The program manager presented a somewhat different focus to the question of center challenges. For example, transportation provided a problem as some girls traveled as much as 20 miles to reach Reel Grrls. Although free bus passes were available, it did not necessarily resolve the transportation issue. Childcare was another challenge. She went on to explain: "We met some kids who were interested in the program and they had babies. Kids with babies. What do you do with teens who have kids? Their moms would babysit for them, but if we want to work with kids who have babies, we need to know about handling daycare."

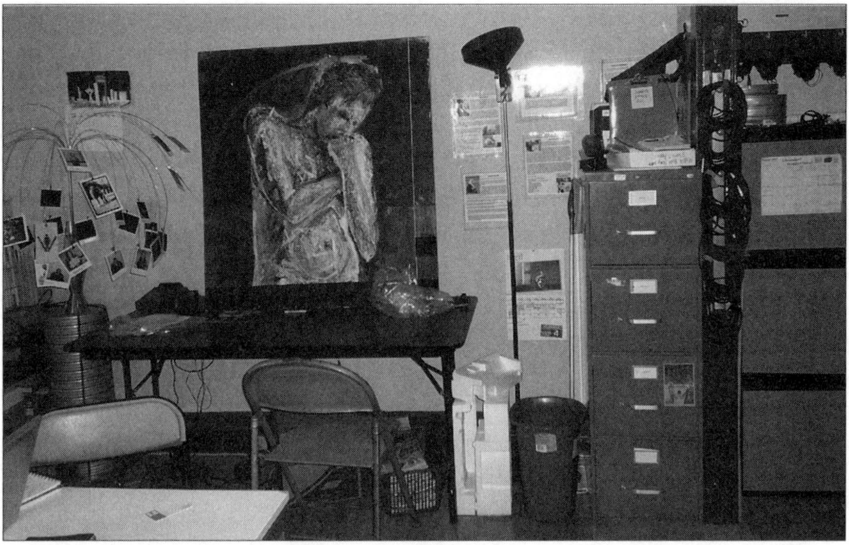

Figure 4.4 The Reel Grrls Office

Of particular concern was the lack of racial diversity in Reel Grrls programming. The program manager suggested that Reel Grrls currently was not attracting enough women of color or women with varied socioeconomic backgrounds, either as staff members or users. The program manager felt that by recruiting more ethnically diverse staff, the teens could be provided with positive role models and more opportunity to work with women of color in the film industry. Developing and fostering this cultural diversity was considered important to the center's future.

Digital Inclusion

Reel Grrls targets users from all socioeconomic and ethnic groups by providing youth media programs that are restricted only by age and gender. It empowers teenage girls with the skills and confidence to tell their stories through film. The organization provides a safe environment for girls to explore their ideas without the intimidation and male judgment typically present in boy-focused or mixed-gender media programs. Augmenting this environment is the trusting attitude embraced by Reel Grrls staff since users are permitted to checkout expensive laptops and video equipment. The fostering of life skills such as responsibility, teamwork, and public speaking helps the girls develop the type of work ethic desired by employers. Moreover, the technology skills they learn in the areas of digital video and audio will also help them to pursue further educational and professional goals.

Reel Grrls is an important vehicle for promoting digital inclusion among at-risk youth populations. Girls who have not worked with digital media or do not have such technical programs available in their schools are encouraged to explore the possibilities offered and encouraged by the program. Reel Grrls makes high-end equipment and myriad software programs available to users from at-risk demographics. Through outreach among homeless, minority, and low-income populations, Reel Grrls strives to provide as many girls with digital media experience as possible.

Endnotes

1. All case study participants have been given aliases for privacy protection.

CHAPTER 5

La Casa Hogar—Bringing Families Into the Community

Carol F. Landry and Rebecca Kuglitsch

La Casa Hogar, a nonprofit agency located in Yakima, Washington, aims to better serve adult immigrant women in the Yakima Valley by providing them with the educational and self-development opportunities they need to adapt to their new environment, gain confidence, and learn to overcome the barriers in their lives. Many of the women are Spanish-speaking with limited education and technology skills. A program of the Yakima Interfaith Coalition, La Casa Hogar was founded in 1995 by Ninfa Gutierrez. At the time of writing, La Casa Hogar shared space with another Yakima Interfaith Coalition program in a repurposed house located in a quiet Yakima city neighborhood (Figure 5.1).

Getting Connected Through La Casa Hogar

An important aspect of the center's education and learning opportunities is its community technology center (CTC). The CTC is comprised of a classroom and small computer lab located on the second floor of the house. English, Spanish, general education, and technology classes take place in the classroom area, with lessons often making use of the computer lab next door. The lab is housed in a long, narrow room painted a soothing light blue. It is lined with desks holding the center's nine Dell computers. Each desk is supplied with a rolling chair, and posted above the workstations are hand-lettered sheets with keyboard commands for producing Spanish characters, such as accented vowels. The computers run the Windows XP operating system and come

Figure 5.1 La Casa Hogar, Yakima, Washington

equipped with the full suite of Office programs. The language application Rosetta Stone is installed for learning English, as is a typing program and a folder of miscellaneous applications and resources devoted to drivers education. All computers have high-speed internet connectivity.

Visiting the CTC

To better understand the benefits of the La Casa Hogar CTC, 10 women were recruited and interviewed over several visits to the center: five employees, one volunteer, and four CTC users. Staff ranged in age from approximately 19 to 55 years. Length of employment at La Casa Hogar varied from less than one year to just over six years, while job responsibilities consisted of administrative and technology support, grant writing, cooking, housekeeping, teaching, and childcare. Users ranged in age from 38 to 57 years, and all gave Spanish as their first language. No user had completed a high school education; two had attended school for six years, one for eight years, and one until she was age 16. None of the users was working at the

Figure 5.2 La Casa Hogar Reception Room

time of the interviews, although three were either seeking employment or had secured future employment. Two participants were fruit pickers who were expecting to work when called, one was seeking employment as a caregiver, and one gave her occupation as a housewife. Finally, user household structures varied, with household sizes ranging from two to five members.

The Women and CTC Use

To obtain a more complete picture of the La Casa Hogar CTC, it was important to first ascertain how the women had learned about the center, how long they had been using the center, and how often they visited the center. Participants indicated that word of mouth brought most of the users to the center; however, friends, family, and service agencies also acted as referring mechanisms. The women indicated that they had been using the center for as little as a few months to as long as seven years. When asked about the amount of time spent at the CTC, the women found it difficult to formulate a response given that attendance was irregular and depended heavily on family and

Figure 5.3 La Casa Hogar CTC

work obligations. When they could attend, they usually came to classes that met for at least two hours a day three times a week, totaling an approximate usage of six hours per week. Carolina, a 38-year-old fruit picker and mother of three, estimated that when she attended classes, she spent six to eight hours a week at the center. Staff confirmed that June to October was a less active period at the center as most users were employed in seasonal fruit-picking during that time.

The purpose of this case study was to investigate the benefits accrued as a result of CTC use. Both staff and users were asked how the women were helped or what they had gained from using the La Casa Hogar CTC. Center impact was evident according to individual, family, and community outcomes.

Individual Benefits

With regard to individual benefits, improved English skills were cited in several cases. Although none of the users was yet comfortable conversing in English, it was mentioned that even learning basic words was helpful. Carolina articulated the importance of learning English when she declared:

> I wanted to better myself ... I wanted to educate myself. Learning English was important. And it's important to learn English to communicate with other people, and to find a better job ... I've developed my English. Little by little, I can ask things and talk in English. I'm learning a little, and I talk more. Also I can find information better now. In the library, I can find it better. It just helps not to be scared.

Echoing this sentiment, 57-year-old Esperanza said that she came to the CTC to learn English because she wanted to communicate better with her family. Esperanza has 12 children, two of whom have graduated from high school and "talk in English, and I don't understand."

The classes offered at the CTC have also helped many women complete their General Educational Development (GED) test. One of the most compelling examples of individual impact came from MaryAnne, the center's cook and housekeeper for the past three years. Although a La Casa Hogar employee, MaryAnne is also a student. Here is her story:

> I lived 27 years in the U.S., over 20 years in Los Angeles. I came here; my daughter was sick. She asked for help. When I came here, I couldn't speak or understand English. [At La Casa Hogar] I start at English level 1. Now I am at level 5. When I finish level 5, I'd like to go to college. I like to be a nurse. Soon I take my GED. I have four kids. I worked for my kids. Now is time for me.

A number of women also used the CTC as a stepping stone to college. By improving their English skills and completing the GED, they were better prepared to pursue college degrees.

Esperanza highlighted another individual benefit of CTC use: learning basic computer skills. She spoke enthusiastically about discovering how to use a computer and was particularly proud of knowing how to type without needing to look at the keyboard. Many of the women spoke of how they came to the CTC with a fear of computers, but center technology classes provided them with the confidence to learn basic skills first and then progress to more advanced topics.

For Laura, a 42-year-old fruit picker, passing her driving test was accredited to the help she received at the La Casa Hogar CTC. By becoming comfortable with a computer and learning how to navigate a computer-based simulation program, Laura was prepared to take and pass the computerized Department of Motor Vehicles test. Many women at La Casa Hogar had found the computerized drivers test impossible to pass prior to attending the CTC. The drivers education instructor Angelina pointed out that, "They understand driving situations by using the computer better than reading a book. It is easier to see and use it when they can't read or write English." Laura, and many more women, were able to obtain their licenses with the help of the La Casa Hogar CTC.

In addition to English as a Second Language, GED, and drivers training applications, the CTC installs the CONEVyT program on its computers. This program provides a type of distance education in which immigrant women can complete various levels of education through the Mexican educational system. The portal is linked to a variety of Mexican agencies such as the National Institute for Adult Education and the Department of Education. Stephany, a computer class assistant who has lived in the U.S. for one-and-a-half years, explained it this way: "It is a program that gives the opportunity to learn over the internet. Some women finish elementary or middle school in Mexico. Some people don't finish [school] in Mexico, but they can through this program." Educational attainment in any language is a positive outcome for the women of La Casa Hogar.

Significantly, the women have benefited from using the CTC through the development of the confidence necessary to pass their drivers tests, learn to speak English, or obtain their GEDs. The center functions as an emotionally supportive and safe environment for them to learn and connect with others.

Family Benefits

The women also talked about the positive family outcomes that emerged from their involvement with the La Casa Hogar CTC. Ana, a 42-year-old newly single mother, said, "From all of this, I bettered my family. All of these classes are so important in improving family life." For some families, the CTC acts as their only access to computers and the internet. The center becomes a vehicle for providing educational support to their children, keeping their families safe, and maintaining connections with family and friends.

The organization's administrator spoke of how school-age children benefited from the center as their mothers were able to help them with homework and computer tasks. She elaborated: "We had a woman with preschool children, and she saw a kid's sheet on the internet and asked if she could print it out to work at home with her kids. So she did, every day, and it was good for her kids."

According to Carolina, the CTC "helps us as a family. It helps my kids that I am losing my fear of my computer. It's a lot better since I can help my kids now." Thanks to her improved English and computer skills, Carolina can provide better educational support for her 17-year-old son and two young daughters. Similarly, the center users indicated that their children were more open to learning because they have an example in their mothers. Carolina, referring to her children, explained, "They feel proud that their mother goes to school."

The CTC at La Casa Hogar also helps keep families safe. Laura, a mother of three including two teenage sons, found classes on gangs extremely helpful. She was familiar with youth getting into trouble in Mexico as well as the U.S., but she did not know about local gangs and how to tell if someone was involved in them until she took classes at the CTC. In addition, some women with home computers found that their lack of knowledge about computers could pose a threat to their children's safety, realizing that their children could potentially be accessing information about pornography, guns, or satanic worship. By learning about computer security and management, La Casa Hogar women could provide increased protection for their families.

The CTC also provides a way to communicate with family and friends, both in the U.S. and back home. This not only promotes technological understanding in the U.S., but also in the home country. The administrator told a story of one user who communicates by web camera with her family in Mexico, stating, "It brings the family to the cyber cafes in Mexico. They learn the computer, and it benefits both places, both parts learn the computer." Not only has the user improved her access to technology, but she has inspired her family in Mexico to take steps toward digital participation by corresponding with her via email and video.

Community and Washington State Benefits

The community experienced many benefits as a result of the women's use of the CTC. According to La Casa Hogar's administrator, "Breaking fear of computers is good for community. There's computers everywhere. ... Women become more self-confident, more able to participate and integrate into community." The English classes taught using CTC computers also facilitate women to speak for themselves within the community. Expressing a similar conviction, Marisol, a grant-writing volunteer, stated that women "feel empowered and valued in their neighborhoods" as a result of skills and confidence developed at the CTC. She went on to explain that some of the women users were forming a community coalition in their neighborhood.

Furthermore, economic conditions improve as English skills improve and women become more comfortable talking with others. Stephany pointed out, "When Mexican people know more of the [U.S.] culture, more language, they get jobs." Better paying jobs may address social concerns such as welfare, taxes, and paying for children's education. Moreover, the state benefits by having a workforce that is not tied to seasonal work but that is able to be employed year round with potentially higher paying jobs.

Challenges Facing La Casa Hogar

Operators of CTCs wish to provide optimum experiences for their users, and La Casa Hogar is no different. Yet challenges and barriers frequently preclude this goal. When asked about such challenges, staff presented a number of issues. Space was the predominant problem for the La Casa Hogar CTC. Classrooms were considered too small when large classes convened. Similarly, there were too few computers. The center had nine computers, but classes often had a compliment of 12–15 people. This resulted in the need to double up on computers, which was looked upon unfavorably by a number of students.

Finding qualified teachers was also a challenge. The center's administrator spoke of the time La Casa Hogar was able to obtain an experienced Yakima Valley Community College teacher for a computer class. However, in order to retain the instructor, they were required to have a minimum of 15 students in the class. The administrator explained:

> At the time, we had eight computers, and we began with 15 students. Students had to share, and some of them didn't like that so they dropped. Then the teacher can't stay because less than 15 students. So then we started with volunteers for

> teachers. Sometimes, no students. Then students would come, no volunteer.

Additionally, too few hours of operation, lack of childcare, and work commitments were seen as barriers to CTC attendance. The center was only open Monday through Friday, yet many women felt that they would be better able to attend on Saturday and Sunday. Children are welcome at La Casa Hogar, but childcare is only provided to those aged 2 to 5 years, although mothers are allowed to keep infants with them at the center. The childcare service did not address the needs of children in other age groups. Work created the most significant barrier to using the CTC for immigrant women. As Laura, a fruit picker, noted, "It's difficult when I want to come and work [at the center]. I lose time when I'm not working [in the orchards] and am here, and that means I lose money."

When asked how the center could be improved or developed in the future, staff felt that providing more space and reliable teachers was the primary way to improve the center. Updated technology was judged important to the center's future. Offering more classes and increasing the hours of operation was also deemed necessary for future CTC development, as this would help meet the disparate schedules of La Casa Hogar's users. Expansion of childcare beyond children age 2 to 5 years was seen as a way to eliminate a considerable barrier and permit more women to benefit from use of the CTC.

Empowerment Through Technology

The La Casa Hogar CTC targets Spanish-speaking immigrant women who typically have low levels of education, limited to nonexistent English language skills, no computer or internet experience, and living in the low-income bracket. Women who have often never used a computer before are prepared at La Casa Hogar for the day-to-day interactions with technology required by life in twenty-first-century Washington State. Users develop language, computer, and driving skills while also completing requirements necessary to obtain their GEDs. All of these skills empower women to speak for themselves both within their families and within the community, and this can lead to material benefits such as increased employment and increased economic status.

As most users do not have either a computer or high-speed internet connectivity in their homes, the La Casa Hogar CTC is often the only place where the women can access such technology. Without the center, many would simply lack the confidence and equipment to be able to participate in the digital world. The classes and instruction given at the CTC help reduce the anxiety and stress associated with technology and help users to take ownership of technology as a part of normal life, thus increasing their inclusion in the digital realm. It gives users a sense of empowerment to be able to use computers and the internet for their informational and educational needs.

The families of the women who use the center are also brought further into the digital world. The women can better support their children's educational goals and technology awareness, finding online resources to encourage preschool children to learn at home and developing skills to aid older children with computer use and internet research. The women become role models for their children, inspiring them to aim high in their educational goals. Computer proficiency allows women to understand how their children are using computers and how to ensure that they are making safe choices in the websites they visit. Furthermore, the CTC at La Casa Hogar is inspiring women to bring technology into their homes. Many of the women spoke of their hopes to learn enough or save enough to purchase a computer with internet access in the future. Some women had already managed to achieve this goal, with La Casa Hogar helping to find computer donors.

In summing up the importance of the La Casa Hogar CTC, the administrator, a former student and now an employee who works with administrative services and technology, said it best when she testified, "I feel happy when I see women come and see it [the computer] for the first time. Then months later they use email to communicate, they break the fear of turning it on, and know they can't break it [computer]." Even if these are quiet accomplishments, they must not be underestimated.

CHAPTER 6

4-H Network News—Teaching Youth to Build Community

Jack Baur and Sonja Sutherland

4-H Network News, part of the 4-H Afterschool Forestry Program in Quilcene, Washington, is described by coordinators as "a youth-run internet multi-media club." The goal of the program is to help teens from this remote rural area develop the technical and communication skills to launch them into a broader cultural context and lead them to feel a wider sense of belonging, so that they will be socially and intellectually ready to transition into college. As a community technology center (CTC), Washington State University (WSU) Jefferson County Extension in Port Hadlock, Washington, provides access to more than 14 computer stations for youth through two co-located WSU programs: 11 computers in the WSU Learning Center North Olympic Peninsula and three computers in the WSU Jefferson County Extension 4-H office. All of these computers are outfitted with Final Cut Pro for editing digital video. Students are also trained on what staff describe as "Hollywood standard, low-end prosumer" grade digital video cameras. Students involved with 4-H Network News collaborate with the local newspaper, the *Port Townsend & Jefferson County Leader*, which posts the 4-H video productions on its online news site. It also covers youth and 4-H related stories for the National 4-H Council, including events such as the Academy of Country Music Awards and the *Charlotte's Web* movie.

4-H is the "youth arm" of the nationwide land-grant university system, federally subsidized institutions that support higher education opportunities throughout rural America. 4-H is the largest youth organization in the country; with almost 7 million members, it is twice as large as the next largest youth organization, Boys & Girls Clubs of America. WSU, Washington State's land-grant institution, supports 4-H Network News through its co-located WSU Jefferson County Extension and WSU Learning Center North Olympic Peninsula. The 4-H Afterschool Forestry Program employs three instructors and one part-time student assistant. Seven adult volunteers also help out on a regular basis. At the time of our visit, there were 40 students involved in various aspects of the program. 4-H Network News was made possible through funds from Title III of the Secure Rural Schools Act of 2000. However, the provision only pays for afterschool programs that are forestry-related; therefore, programs must meet this requirement.

An early example of 4-H work was modeled after an online news show called Rocketboom (www.rocketboom.com). For this project, students chose a newspaper article about a local issue, read the article, filmed some "b-roll" footage, and provided commentary. In time, teens began attending community events and conducting interviews with event participants for Network News. Other projects included online news reporting for the U.S. Forest Service and the Washington

Figure 6.1 4-H Learning Center

State Governor's Office, as well as partnerships with the Bill & Melinda Gates Foundation, Northwest Area Foundation, National 4-H Council, WSU's Center to Bridge the Digital Divide, Kiwanis, Port Hadlock Chamber of Commerce, Rotary International, and various news organizations in Seattle. 4-H youth have covered events in Seattle, such as Folklife and the Capitol Hill Block Party, as well as the Washington State Fair in Puyallup and Academy of Country Music Awards in Las Vegas.

Figure 6.2 4-H Computer Lab

The importance of this program and its CTC to local teens cannot be understated. According to the coordinator of the 4-H program, poverty, drugs, and alcohol abuse are common in Quilcene. Having worked as the principal of the Quilcene school, she is intimately aware of the severity of these problems as numerous youth were removed from their homes due to abuse issues during her tenure. Amid this tumultuous social environment, she sees the goal of 4-H Network News as building students' confidence and leadership abilities by teaching them technology skills. The 4-H coordinator goes on to say, "We're looking at leadership through different strands, and technology is one of them … we tell the kids, 'you are the hope in your communities.'"

Meeting the Staff and Users

Since the intent of this case study was to examine the 4-H CTC for positive outcomes linked to its use, we spoke with staff members via a conference call and held a focus group with teenage users. All users were students, ranging in age from 14 to 16 years, and were from households comprised of three to five members. Of the staff, the 4-H coordinator has worked at the center for five years, while the WSU Learning Center coordinator has been employed there for the past 10 years. We also observed center activity. Since 4-H Network News is set up as an after-school program and as summer technology camps in June and August, few kids were present during the researchers' visit.

The Youth of 4-H CTC and Network News

To learn more about the 4-H CTC and its users, researchers inquired how the youth came to learn about the center, how long they have been using it, and what drew them to the CTC. The youth reported that they learned about the center from the 4-H coordinator, who actively recruits teens for the program. CTC use varied from 2 to 4 years, and attendance fluctuated with program offerings; however, when programs were in session, visits were generally 1 to 2 days per week. Network News was the primary attraction drawing kids to the CTC, but doing homework and learning about photography, video editing, and website design as well as an assortment of other computer applications were also cited as desirable activities. All users indicated that they have access to computers and the internet at home, with one youth having a dial-up connection and the others DSL connectivity.

Individual Benefits

When asked how individuals have benefited from their association with the 4-H CTC, compelling responses were obtained from both staff and CTC users. For example, teens develop a sense of confidence in their abilities based on the skills and experiences accumulated over time with the program. As verification of this fact, the 4-H coordinator

Figure 6.3 Teleconferencing Video Equipment in 4-H Computer Lab

related a story about some 4-H Network News youth who attended an academic high school summer camp at WSU called Cougar Quest. The students' experiences at this camp allowed them to see that the technology skills they had developed through 4-H Network News were just as good, if not better, than students coming from more affluent areas of the state. The 4-H coordinator stated that this realization has helped them feel more confident about their abilities, and this added confidence will help encourage them to continue with their education.

Confidence is a tremendous outcome for children living in this poor, rural community; however, in order to build self-belief, concrete skills must first be acquired and refined. The coordinators strive to give teens the opportunity to take on the various roles in the production of a news program—videography, film editing, photography, reporting, and more—by requiring them to spend time working in each of the positions. As a result, 14-year-old Colin, a student who has been in 4-H for 2 years, has learned video editing using a Mac application called Final Cut Pro, a digital editing suite, as well as photo editing and HTML. In addition to these programs, John, a 16-year-old student who has used the CTC for the past 4 years, has also learned how to use cascading style sheets (CSS) and JavaScript. Both teens believe that their futures will depend on computers and technology. To illustrate this point, John stated that, "this is the age of computers and you need to know about computers," while another student proclaimed that, "even in the grocery stores, they're not going to have checkers. They're going to have computers."

Sue, who has been using the CTC since the seventh grade, recognized that benefits extend beyond skill development. She contends that she has benefited from the networking outcome as well. Sue explained that, "I gained a network with other people who have the same interests." She then went on to tell about an experience she had last year in which her instructor accompanied a group of students on a trip to Seattle. This instructor had made a connection with someone from the Seattle-based newspaper, *The Stranger*, and brought the teens to meet and interview newspaper staff, along with members of a number of hip music bands. It was an opportunity Sue found exciting on its own merit, but it also allowed her to meet and interact with members of a professional media community. Networking is an important skill to acquire, as it can be applied to any profession and, therefore, is an important outcome for the users of the 4-H CTC.

Family Benefits

In addition to the individual outcomes associated with the CTC, family benefits were noted. For example, users revealed how their experience with technology aided family members by connecting them to technology. Sue said that she helps her father use their computer at home and, in particular, helps him order the things he wants to purchase through the internet. Similarly, Colin indicated that he helps his parents by showing them how to drop photographs from their digital camera's memory card into a computer file. Going beyond distinct families, the 4-H coordinator presented a more complete picture of the connecting families to technology outcome. She states that the youth love to share what they have learned, often helping family members with work on computers at home. Moreover, parents who might not otherwise be inclined to use computers are encouraged to go online to see what their children have been working on with 4-H Network News. She mentioned that parents and family members often come to her wanting physical copies of the web stories because they do not know how to find them online. In these cases, she usually sits down with the family members at a computer, shows them how to access the group's webpage, and invites them to ask their students for more assistance, beginning a conversation about technology and the internet in the home.

Families also appreciate the safe environment that the 4-H CTC presents. When recruiting students to participate in the center programs, the 4-H coordinator contacts parents, talking to them about the activities and the skills that participants will develop. She feels that the nationally recognized 4-H name is one reason for the parents' enthusiasm. They know that their children will have good experiences and, very importantly, will be safe and cared for. Demonstrating this concern for the students' well-being, staff expended significant effort to provide after-school snacks. Initially, this endeavor was stymied by local government regulations. Specifically, 4-H was not permitted to use government funds to purchase snacks for the youth in the after-school program, which was a problem since the youth were coming straight from school and were hungry. However, following some discussion with the county staff and county commissioners, 4-H succeeded in getting an exception to this rule.

Community Benefits

Without a doubt, outcomes related to the 4-H CTC and Network News go well beyond that of the individual and family. The community has experienced tremendous benefits as well. The 4-H coordinator points to the technology-related project in which students made Blogger accounts and webpages for more than 200 local businesses. Although little has been done with the initial webpages, business owners have the rudiments for building a larger web presence for their enterprises, an opportunity that may not have occurred without the aid of the CTC users. Furthermore, 4-H youth can be called upon to enrich the existing web content for a small fee. This mutually beneficial relationship would allow kids to continue building technical skills while providing local establishments with the services of low-cost web development.

In addition to providing local business with an online presence, John employed his technology competencies in other areas. Using his video skills, he helped the high school set up a graduation ceremony slide show. While this 4-H youth was reluctant to "brag" about his skills, the 4-H coordinator did reveal that John also used GPS/GIS technology to map the location of noxious weeds in the national forest while working with the Noxious Weeds Eradication Program. Since noxious weeds are not native to Washington State and are highly destructive and difficult to manage once established, this contribution by a 4-H CTC user represents a significant outcome for the forestry service as well as the community-at-large. Student John provided them with a tool to aid in the control of harmful plants.

On a more abstract level, the 4-H coordinator sees the activities of the youth as encouraging community cohesion while building technological infrastructure. She feels the youth are "giving voice to positive messages and under-represented voices" in the community by placing particular focus on youth, rural community members, and racial minorities in their stories. The 4-H coordinator also points out that the youth themselves become a story as they are working on their news projects, which arouses community pride while exposing areas in which communication technologies can be used to build further community networks.

Challenges and Future Development

Despite the program's successes, the 4-H coordinator says there are a few factors that have made it difficult for some youth to participate. One of these is a lack of time. Because they live in a small community, the youth become involved with many different after-school programs as they move into high school, such as cheerleading and football. This makes it harder to schedule time for 4-H Network News.

Another difficulty to overcome was perception: When 4-H Network News started, area teens apparently thought that 4-H was "uncool and for little kids." The 4-H coordinator worked to change this mindset by actively recruiting teens who others perceived as "cool" to become involved in the video program. Once the program gained acceptance and popularity, it was opened up to more students. She says that the initial year of social engineering with the six "cool" students was crucial in building up a solid reputation with teens and that the program could not have been as successful or popular without this.

Additionally, for some of the youth, the distance that they must travel to get to the WSU complex is a major barrier. It is a 30-minute drive one way to Port Hadlock from Quilcene, and they are not always able to get transportation. 4-H has helped to mitigate this problem somewhat through the purchase of a retired van from Jefferson County Transit. They have been able to use this van to transport students to and from the WSU complex.

The county also questioned the amount of money that was being spent on equipment for the program, particularly when it came to purchasing the expensive cameras. The county did not understand how buying cameras could possibly meet the requirement of being forestry-related; however, once they saw how successful the program was, resistance melted away. These cameras are also available to lend to adults and schools in the community when they are not in use by 4-H Network News.

From the users' perspective, time was the greatest challenge to using the CTC and participating in 4-H Network News. For John, who lived farther away, this included the added time required to get to and from the WSU site. The students were then asked directly if there were any negative social implications for participating in 4-H. They assured researchers that there was not. Apparently the 4-H coordinator efforts to make 4-H cool have been successful.

Branching Outwards

It is clear from the interviews that the program is a success. The students involved in 4-H are offered a variety of experiences that help build their sense of civic responsibility, confidence, and self-worth, and they are also being equipped with valuable technology skills far beyond what would normally be acquired in high school. This occurs in a supportive environment in which a strong value is placed on higher education and academic success. Additionally, they and other members of the community are given access to a well-equipped computing center that places an emphasis on economic development and communication technology.

The CTC staff want to make sure the teens in their area receive a solid base of instruction and practical experience working with technology. They note that because these students live in a rural area, they tend to internalize the notion that they would not be capable of successfully completing college. It is for this reason that the staff is particularly concerned with finding ways to show the teens they are capable of succeeding when competing with their urban and suburban peers.

One of the ways they do this is by teaching the students computer and digital video skills, and another is by giving them the opportunity to compare what they've learned with what their peers know—as in the case of Cougar Quest.

Both the 4-H coordinator and the WSU Learning Center coordinator feel that their collaboration could be used as a model for other organizations—locally, nationally, and internationally. Indeed, the international attention that they have already received speaks volumes about their success. The benefits that have been felt not only by the direct participants but radiating throughout the community suggest that, properly implemented, similar programs could enjoy success around the world. The focus within Jefferson County 4-H is on maintaining a sense of purpose, rather than getting "too widgety"—not getting hung up on individual, specific projects or technologies but keeping a clear mission of providing a safe place for kids to explore technology and the way that it can be used to connect them to the world. They want these teens to see themselves as active players in life, not just cogs in the wheel of bureaucracy. By thinking big, they have been able to do more with the resources at their disposal as well as to keep their vision moving forward.

CHAPTER 7

Tacoma Clubhouse—Helping Students Succeed

Rebecca Kuglitsch, Meghan Madonna, and Sophy Johnston

The Tacoma Clubhouse, a branch of the Intel Computer Clubhouse (ICC) system, provides at-risk youth (ages 10 through 18) in the largely African-American Hilltop area of Tacoma, Washington, with access to computers and technology training. The clubhouse, which was founded in 1999 with grants from the Bill & Melinda Gates Foundation and the Intel Corporation, is currently hosted by Allen Renaissance, Inc., an affiliate of the Allen African Methodist Episcopal church. According to the 2000 U.S. Census, 22 percent of Hilltop residents are living below the poverty line. The clubhouse founder and coordinator stated that all of its users live below the poverty line, 50 percent live in transient situations, and 25 percent are homeless.

Tacoma Clubhouse offers local youth a creative and safe environment to develop media interests and technology skills but also focuses on helping them build confidence and leadership abilities. Its four main programs are an after-school open computer lab where users can work on creative projects with peers and mentors; an all-girl math, science, and engineering program; an all-boy math, science, and engineering program; and a program that trains youth to become A+ Certified computer technicians. Because clubhouse leaders believe it is important to have technology tools available at all times, the clubhouse lends laptops to users, and its mentors assist users in purchasing technology. In addition to technology training, users can receive social agency referrals, get meals, and obtain help with job and college searches and applications.

The clubhouse is situated in a former store, surrounded by abandoned buildings. Windows are decorated with brightly painted plywood cutouts of young people, possibly to discourage vandalism. As one user indicated, he had arrived particularly early that day as some "kids" who were not in the program had been hanging around wanting to "break in and do stupid stuff like kids do." User excitement and engagement with the program became apparent as they rushed into the center when the doors opened to claim one of the 20 available computers.

Who We Interviewed

To better understand the impact of the Tacoma Clubhouse, researchers spoke with the clubhouse founder and coordinator and conducted a focus group with five youth users. The founder had been working at the ICC since its inception in 1999. Of the focus group participants, three were male and two female. Users ranged in age from 14 to 16 years (average 15.2 years). All five identified as students, gave English as their first language, and live in households of two to six members. Researchers also observed people using the clubhouse.

Figure 7.1 User Alley Entrance to the Tacoma Clubhouse

Figure 7.2 Official Entrance on Martin Luther King Jr. Way

Who Are the Users?

To comprehend how the Tacoma Clubhouse affects the community and its members, researchers needed to determine how youth had learned about the clubhouse, how frequently they visited it, and how long they had been coming to the center. Participants stated that family or friends recommended the clubhouse, which they have been attending between 2 months to 3 years, and visits were approximately 3 days per week. User interests varied from music and technology to photography and video production to repairing computers. Similarly, users had tried myriad activities, including computer programming, acting as mentors to other kids, building webpages, and learning computer applications such as Photoshop and LEGO Robotics.

Individual Benefits

When asked how individuals had been helped as a result of using the center, the clubhouse coordinator indicated that many of the students were doing better in school and were more motivated to go to college or seek employment in technical fields: "At least 50 percent of

Figure 7.3 Clubhouse Rules

the users have gone on to college, 10 to 15 percent currently work in technical fields, and the rest are still around working in a technical environment." All the youth who had been using the clubhouse for 1–3 years had shown academic improvement. Sixteen-year-old LaKeesha told how the center helped with her math skills: "Before I never got more than a B, now I got an A." Thirteen of the current clubhouse users were working in technical internships and contract positions for their summer break. Of particular note is the 11-year-old clubhouse user who became Microsoft's youngest intern. These opportunities are facilitated by staff who provide referrals, write letters of recommendation, and introduce kids to influential community leaders.

Concomitantly, users developed greater confidence regarding their job skills, which was clearly demonstrated when asked about their occupations—not one interviewee listed "student' as his or her occupation but rather cited computer programmer, teacher, technician, and musician instead. Similarly, 15-year-old LeRoy expressed confidence as he described his improved approach to troubleshooting computer problems: "[Before, I] never knew how to use a computer, I used to get in fights with it, slap it around when it didn't work, but now I know what to do." LaKeesha, a center user for 2 years, articulated self-assurance when speaking of Photoshop: "I knew nothing about Photoshop, now I use it all the time." Fourteen-year-old James was pleased that he is now able to "build my own software." Some of the students have learned how to design and build websites, and others have utilized software programs, such as Scratch, which facilitate the creation of interactive stories, games, animation, and music. And still more have learned how to use video editing software such as Pico Met.

Significantly, the leadership outcome is visible among users as the center works to foster future community leaders. Demonstrating this point, the clubhouse coordinator testified the following: "Kids often come back to volunteer and/or give back to the community. They [the clubhouse] operate under a model of service by teaching the idea of *Sankofa*—an African term for going back to get someone as you climb."

Echoing this sentiment, Orlando, who has used the center for the past three years, stated: "We learn and are taught a lot of things here, then give back to the community. I would like to give back more." Students can be promoted to the clubhouse board and become teaching assistants or assistant coordinators. They are also given the opportunity to teach technology skills at local middle and elementary schools. All of the lessons and skills that youth learn at the clubhouse place them on a pathway to success.

According to the clubhouse coordinator, the skills they learn at the center go beyond the technological: "All of the programs are interdisciplinary and the kids learn integrated skills using different applications and solving complex problems. This produces well-rounded kids. They have to troubleshoot when the technology doesn't work and try to solve the problem."

Family Benefits

Users feel that their families have also benefited from their attendance at the center. For instance, participants are able to pass on the skills they have learned to those at home, connecting their families to technology. LaKeesha explained, "I got to teach my sister and Mom how to use some stuff on computers." Families can also experience an improved family atmosphere. Adam's dad showed increased pride in his son, complimenting him on how responsible he had become since attending the Tacoma Clubhouse, while Pam's grandmother also felt that she had gained a sense of responsibility through clubhouse activities.

Families benefit from the safety outcome engendered by the center. The clubhouse coordinator explained: "Parents can come in to be with kids while they're learning. Parents can volunteer at events. They can be involved, know what the kids are doing, and know that their kids are in a safe place." Such assurance regarding the safety of one's children may be difficult to attain otherwise in the challenging environment of Tacoma's Hilltop neighborhood.

Community Benefits

In addition to helping individuals and families, the Tacoma Clubhouse provides positive outcomes for the community. In fact, giving back to the community is a critical element of the center's philosophy. Referring back to the concept of *Sankofa*, youth learn how to participate successfully in their communities. For example, clubhouse users created promotional videos and E as a Second Language tutorials for the Tacoma Community House, a nonprofit organization that provides assistance to local immigrant communities. This provided low-cost resources for the organization to help immigrants learn English. Some of these immigrants were then trained in technical programs at the clubhouse and went on to work at the clubhouse. Students in the A+ Certificate program fix computers for local businesses and organizations. Community members who otherwise might not have been able to afford such services reap benefits while students gain the opportunity to improve their knowledge, gain real-life experience, and interact with their surrounding world.

Many users continue this tradition of community participation as adults, returning to become clubhouse mentors or going on to volunteer in other local organizations. Youth are also encouraged to look beyond their locality and think globally. On one project, center users and staff raised money for a trip to Ghana where they visited a Liberian refugee camp and provided internet connections and computer assistance to residents.

On a more fundamental level, the community benefits because kids are engaged in productive activities rather than creating problems on the street. Reflecting this outcome, James stated that "before I had too much free time and got into trouble. Now, I learn to do stuff." The clubhouse keeps James, and many more like him, occupied and off the streets.

Clubhouse Challenges

When asked about the challenges or difficulties encountered with center use, the kids did not see any problems. Orlando commented that no matter what query he has, there is always someone at the clubhouse who can provide him with answers. Pam pointed out that there were no transportation obstacles that prevented center use because all of the kids lived close by. Orlando explained: "If students want to explore new avenues at the clubhouse, they can simply let the coordinator know and she will make it possible." As an example, he spoke about the time that Adam expressed an interest in learning to fix computers, and the coordinator responded by setting up the A+ Certificate program for computer technicians. LeRoy concluded by giving the coordinator credit for "always ask[ing] us and involve[ing] us in leadership."

Although the Tacoma Clubhouse receives generous support from many avenues, money is always a challenge for nonprofit organizations. The coordinator informed us that ICC is currently renovating a larger building in order to expand its operations but that funding is still needed for this project. Ideally, the clubhouse founder and coordinator would like to develop the center into a series of campuses where each of the four programs could have its own designated space. She would like to create more and stronger partnerships with schools, colleges, and local businesses. She would also like to offer nontechnical services at the center such as social services, mental health, medical and dental aid, and services for transients and gang members. She believes that an endowment could be crucial to the growth of the center, stating that they need "a financial support system so that the financial burden isn't central to the mission."

The Bigger Picture

Digital inclusion is strongly fostered by the programs at the Tacoma Clubhouse. Youth who would have been traditionally underrepresented in the technical community now conceptualize themselves as technically savvy and members of that professional community. The efforts of the center to bring technology to the homes of users, and the positive recommendations of users to their families and friends, create a kind of viral marketing system that operates as an effective way of spreading the digital message. As the teens are valued members of the community, their words about the clubhouse and the digital world in general are more trustworthy to the community than the encouragement of external authority figures. Thus, the digital divide is addressed both immediately and in the long term through the hard work and dedication of organizations such as Tacoma Clubhouse.

CHAPTER 8

Yesler Terrace Community Center—Growing Out of Poverty

Maggie Hardiman and Barbara McKnight

The Yesler Terrace Community Center, remodeled in 2005, is a bright and welcoming space where community members come together daily to interact and socialize. The center encompasses a multitude of services including a community technology center (CTC), teen center, fitness room, gymnasium and basketball court, multipurpose room, childcare center, and a commons area. The community center is part of Yesler Terrace, the oldest public housing development in Washington State. Administered by the Seattle Housing Authority, Yesler Terrace is one of many developments that aims to fulfill the organization's mission of enhancing the Seattle community "by creating and sustaining decent, safe and affordable living environments that foster stability and self-sufficiency for people with low incomes" (www.seattlehousing.org). Today, Yesler Terrace houses approximately 1,500 low-income, ethnically diverse residents living in 561 apartments. The community center is centrally located on Yesler Way so that all residents may have easy access. The center's hours of operation vary, but it remains open until 9:00 PM Monday through Friday and until 5:00 PM on Saturday.

The Yesler CTC

The CTC was established in 2000 with the help of funding from Seattle Public Libraries. It houses 18 computers, each equipped with high-speed internet access. Mornings are dedicated to an assortment of classes that are intended to reach out to the diverse resident

Figure 8.1 Yesler Community Center Sign

population. Classes include English as a Second Language (ESL), computer basics, senior classes, teen multimedia classes, and homework tutoring, along with a special class targeting children participating in a nearby Head Start program. From September through June, six to eight classes are offered each month for adults and seniors; however, afternoons are devoted to an open lab, where people can sign up to use a computer for a 1-hour time slot. Once his or her allotted hour has passed, the person may continue to use the computer if no one else is waiting.

The lab also includes a staff workstation, with two chairs nearby to use while chatting to staff or waiting for a computer to become available. The director of the CTC works with organizations such as Harborview Neighborhood House and Seattle Public Housing to raise funds for the CTC's operations.

The Yesler Visits

To understand more about the Yesler Terrace CTC, researchers made a number of visits to the center to meet with staff members and users. Focus groups were comprised of students ranging in age from 13 to

Figure 8.2 Yesler Community Center

16 years, with two females and four males in the first group and six males making up the second group. Two adult users were also interviewed: Joe, a 56-year-old unemployed male, and Sandra, a 60-year-old retiree. All users gave English as their first language, and household size varied from one to 10 members (average 4.4).

Three staff were also interviewed. The CTC director had worked at the center for 7 years. Lisa, the teen center's recreation leader, came to the organization 4 months before, while Omar, who had been using the CTC at the community center since he was 11 years old, had been hired that same month to supervise the computer lab. Each visit to the CTC included observation of the users and facility.

Making Use of Yesler

The people who use the Yesler Terrace CTC represent a diverse population. The director spoke of how youth, senior citizens, immigrants, and low-income residents all use the lab, mentioning that the CTC is open to anyone, whether they live in the development or not. Omar, the CTC assistant, pointed out that the majority of users were young people, particularly between the ages of 7 to 14, and that most come in every day. When asked, many of the student participants did not recall when they started using the technology center, although a significant portion had used the lab in the old community center and continued to use the new lab upon its opening in 2005. Joe stated that he had been coming to the computer center for approximately 3 years, while Sandra indicated that she had been using the lab for the past 4 years.

Staff felt that the multipurpose nature of the center was its biggest advantage, explaining that it addressed the needs of the entire community by offering something for everyone. They value it as a place for residents to come and do a variety of activities such as browsing the internet or completing online job applications. The type of information sought by users was generally age dependent. Younger kids tended to use the computers to do homework and online research, play games, communicate with friends on social networking sites such as MySpace and Facebook, and download music. Middle-aged adults wanted to improve life skills, their housing situation, and job prospects. Seniors, on the other hand, came to communicate with friends and family, send and receive pictures of their children and grandchildren, and use websites such as eBay and craigslist for online shopping.

Time spent at the CTC ranged from a few minutes per day to 16–20 hours per week. Kids tended to visit the center more during the school year. Sandra relayed that she did not use the center as much as she would like because there were fewer morning hours available, whereas Joe came to the technology center at least three days per week.

In general, most participants had computer and internet access elsewhere. Home, school, libraries, and the senior center were listed as other locations; however, home computers were typically considered old and connection speeds too slow. Confirming this notion, one teen exclaimed that the dial-up system at home "takes like an hour to connect!" Financial constraints hampered computer upgrades for Joe and Sandra. Joe explained that he is currently in a financial rut and has "no source of income for a while."

Individual Benefits

From the interviews and focus groups, positive outcomes associated with the use of the Yesler Terrace CTC were abundant on an individual level. One such outcome addressed employment, with the CTC offering a place for people to complete job applications. For example, when a number of people had expressed an interest in working at Harborview Hospital, which required them to submit an online job application, they were able to find the technology and guidance they needed at the CTC. The center also facilitates job searching and resume writing. The CTC director spoke of how community agencies such as Job Connections and Seattle Housing Authority send customers to the center to get help "with a quick resume." Employment benefits, too, may be as unassuming as obtaining directions. Again from the director, "Yesterday, I helped a person trying to get a food handler permit. He needed to go to Burien. [To get there], the bus had many transfers on a long and confusing route. After getting help at the center, he was able to get there and passed the [required] test." Because he had used the CTC, this user was now equipped with the documents he needed to obtain a food industry job.

Education was also highlighted as an important individual outcome. Youth use the computer lab to do their homework, and as Omar, the CTC assistant, pointed out, this often leads to better grades in school. Additionally, staff have helped prepare middle school children to succeed in and complete high school and have helped teens to apply for and succeed in college. Lisa, a teen mentor, spoke of a woman who "is very involved with the community but she didn't finish high school, so she is coming in to check how to get her GED." Still more users have improved their English skills through availing themselves of the center's, computers, an important outcome in a housing development with a high immigrant population.

Yesler Terrace CTC also facilitates users to stay in touch with family and friends by allowing them to communicate electronically with others. One youth participant indicated that he spent 15 minutes per day accessing email. Another told how she preferred to do homework at home but used center computers for email or social networking sites like MySpace. Sandra spoke of how she was happy to have learned how to attach documents to email, as she could now send pictures of herself and her son to other members of her family. Supporting such user statements, a staff member conveyed that the primary reason people come to the center is to check email and communicate.

Family Benefits

Staff also felt that the Yesler CTC had a favorable impact on the families of users. They elaborated that parents can be sure their children are safe at the center because they are constantly monitored by staff. The director explained, "I have a good relationship with parents. Kids come here from school. Their parents come to see them and pick them up so I work with the parents and interact with them. If I see a problem, I discuss it with them. I know the kids for 4-plus years. Parents are also taking classes. I talk directly with the kids and have a good relationship with the parents." Omar told of how the CTC can bring families closer together, "I've seen family members use the computer lab. Mom and daughter are spending time in the computer lab so it is together time even if they are working on their own."

Families experience a benefit from the employment outcome as well. As people find work, the extra earnings help these low-income households meet the basic needs of day-to-day living. Furthermore, many families now have access to computer and internet technology as a result of the CTC. As Omar succinctly put it, "[the CTC] allows free computer access without the stress of having to buy a computer."

Community Benefits

The community also benefits from the Yesler Terrace CTC as it provides a welcoming place for community members to gain access to computers and the internet. According to Lisa, "The computer lab is open to the public unless it is class time. Anybody can come in. If so and so needs to do research, it doesn't matter if they are from Yesler. It's free and open to everybody."

Additionally, improved ESL skills correspond to a community communication outcome, as immigrants are better able to speak to employers and co-workers, thereby making work environments less stressful for all involved. It also allows people to speak for themselves rather than having to rely on translators when interacting with government agencies, school officials, or healthcare professionals.

Keeping children safe and off the streets also results in increased security for the community. Lisa points out that "teens get in trouble between 3 PM and 6 PM ... they are loud, but they are here." Consequently, the community benefits by requiring fewer resources to address teenage problems such as crime and vandalism.

The Future of Yesler's CTC

Although the center has been a huge success, there are also challenges. Staff highlighted limited resources, too few operation hours, and limited staffing as difficulties that the center comes up against. When asked what challenges users face while using the center, all three staff members suggested that the language barriers for non-English speaking users were significant. Lisa stated, "If everything is in English and I don't read English that would be very challenging. It would help to have programs from other languages. Immigrants can be some of the smartest people in their homeland. If you don't understand the language, it can be so frustrating. Once that barrier is down, they learn, and we can learn from their culture and that is beautiful." The director also mentioned that senior users face mobility challenges and that the center does not currently have enough resources to optimally reach disabled users.

Similarly, staff felt increased staffing, increased hours of operation, and more computers and software could greatly improve the center. Staff also expressed a desire to develop more inter-maturational programming, for example, teens teaching adults and younger children about new media and technology, and adults tutoring teens on professional skills and practices. Staff felt that all of this could happen with more financial and material resources.

From the users' perspectives, participants in both focus groups felt that having a faster internet connection would improve the service offered by the CTC. Filtering was also mentioned as a barrier to technology use, since it blocked websites that users were trying to access for entertainment and social networking purposes or sometimes sites that contained information that was required for school projects.

Some users in the first focus group felt that a minimum age requirement for using the CTC would improve the level of service, suggesting that 7 years old was a good number. Elaborating on this idea, Sandra felt that there should be separate times for adult users and younger users, as she considered some kids to be too noisy and disruptive. For Joe, more advanced classes for adult users would be useful along with a greater array of software so users could play around with new programs on their own. He did acknowledge, however, that many people are wary of new technology, which could prevent them from utilizing the software available. Conversely, Sandra would like additional morning hours made available for general use since these were the best hours to fit her schedule. At the time of the interview, morning hours were often reserved for classes.

Increasing Inclusion

The Yesler Terrace CTC was established to meet the needs of a diverse community of low-income users. By making free access to computers and the internet available, the CTC facilitates digital inclusion by enabling users to complete homework and research projects, search for and obtain jobs through an online process, and remain connected with family and friends. It empowers immigrants to improve English skills while simultaneously giving them a voice in the wider community. Families can engage with one another as they learn to use technology together. Furthermore, it improves individual and community safety by providing a secure, fun place for teenagers and children to hang out and learn. Perhaps most importantly, the CTC provides the community with a place to access technology, an opportunity that many Yesler CTC users lack elsewhere in their lives.

CHAPTER 9

Washington CASH—Building Financial Assets

Sophy Johnston and Esther Benson

Washington Community Alliance for Self-Help (Washington CASH) is a microenterprise nonprofit organization, founded in Seattle in 1995, that empowers low-income populations to launch successful small businesses. Washington CASH is the only micro-lending organization in Washington that focuses specifically on low-income groups. The agency primarily reaches out to women, who make up 81 percent of its users, although it also targets people with disabilities and other underserved populations including immigrants and refugees. The CASH services are offered to clients free of charge, but all users must qualify as coming under 200 percent of the federal poverty line in order to join the program.

The Washington CASH program is designed in three phases. Participants begin by completing an eight-session business development training course that covers subjects such as developing a business plan, marketing and advertising a business, and record-keeping skills. Before beginning phase one, users complete a technology assessment to measure their level of technical competency.

Once clients have completed the training course, they enter phase two of the program, in which they are placed into business support groups that meet twice monthly. Through these groups, clients are facilitated to apply for microloans ranging from $1,000 to $5,000 to help them begin building their enterprise. Washington CASH maintains that one of the key successes of the program is its peer lending policy. Unless all participants within a group are current with their loan payments, no one else in that group may take out a new loan.

Putting people into such groups creates an automatic support system, because members encourage each other to follow through with their business plans and motivate each other to pay off their loans. In this phase, Washington CASH also matches participants with business mentors, people from the local community who have created successful, sustainable businesses.

In the final phase of the program, the new entrepreneurs gain one-on-one and group assistance with the day-to-day challenges of running their business. Participants also have the option of opening an Individual Development Account, a savings account that is offered in collaboration with United Way of King County, in which participants can contribute up to $2,000. The amount they save is then matched 2-1 with federal funding.

Technology at Washington CASH

One important service that Washington CASH provides to these small-business owners is its community technology center (CTC). The center is open a total of 46 hours per week, with an open lab in operation five of those days. The lab stays open late, until 8:30 PM or 9 PM on Tuesdays, and a technology expert is present one day each week so that users can get help with specific queries they may have. Classes are also offered at the center, in conjunction with the three program phases outlined earlier. Although there is a class introducing users to the basics of computers, most of the business classes also integrate computer skills into their curricula. For example, participants use Word to develop a business plan, use Excel to complete cash flow projections, and learn web design to make a website to promote and advertise their company.

Washington CASH is located in a newer YMCA building that also houses several other organizations providing services to women and youth. Its headquarters consists of a business suite with four offices arranged around the periphery of a large open space. It is in this open space that the CTC is situated, along with a conference table where people can sit and talk. The CTC itself houses five desktop computers, a number of laptops, and two printers. The computers are arranged along one wall of the office suite with windows that look out onto the surrounding neighborhood. There is no privacy, as the computer screens face out into the open communal space, though it does make for a good, if small, instructional space.

Meeting With Staff and Users

To learn about the benefits of Washington CASH's CTC, researchers made two visits to the organization to interview staff and users. On the first visit, the program coordinator of the organization was interviewed. She had worked at Washington CASH for more than a year and was in charge of managing assets, developing classes for the center, occasionally teaching classes, and managing the Individual Development Accounts. The researchers returned to the CASH offices to interview center users. Observation of the center was also carried out.

The Business of Washington CASH

To understand more about the users of the Washington CASH CTC, researchers asked about the reasons people came to the center, how they learned about it, and how often they attend. The program coordinator stated that the number of users at Washington CASH varied month to month, but typically about seven people will come to each class during the week, and a total of 25 people are currently participating in classes. She explained that many users come to Washington CASH with a hobby or idea about a business and want to learn how to turn that interest into a sustainable income, going on to say that users most often need information on marketing and the financial aspects of running a business. Although some users have computers at home, many of these computers are old and operate slowly, or if they have internet access, it is generally limited to dial-up. The coordinator noted that many users lack even basic computer skills.

When asked how she had learned about Washington CASH and the CTC, Sylvia reported that she heard about the center and its services via word of mouth. At the time of the interview, Sylvia was participating in the first phase of the Washington CASH program and was working on completing the business training course. She originally started attending to learn more about small business opportunities, such as marketing, networking, and using a computer for business purposes. Sylvia stated that she was attracted to the organization because she heard it did a good job of teaching people everything they need to know to start their own business. Unlike many of the other users, she indicated that she did have access to a computer and the internet at home. She comes to Washington CASH every other Saturday for her peer support group and attends computer classes whenever she has the time.

Individual Benefits

Without question, Washington CASH and its CTC have provided users with concrete and usable skills. According to the program coordinator, the technology skills learned at the organization are immediately useful. After attending just one workshop, a user may have completed her own business card or gotten a good start on designing and constructing a business website. Supporting this notion, Sylvia pointed out that she "had learned a lot in the computer classes," as she had taken basics in Microsoft Office applications such as Word and Excel and reported that she was now able to write up cost projections in Excel.

Equally important to Sylvia were the networking opportunities provided by encounters with other small business owners and CTC users. By establishing beneficial relationships with other business-oriented people, users benefited from exchanging business tips, ideas, and giving and receiving support. Sylvia felt that these experiences had been crucially important in establishing her enterprise.

Family Benefits

Benefits to families were equally as apparent. The program coordinator reported that the business owners who become established through Washington CASH have a positive impact on their families. By providing positive role models to family members, users can help shape attitudes regarding employment by demonstrating that achieving goals is possible. This is particularly significant to disadvantaged children growing up in impoverished neighborhoods. Additionally, families benefited from the extra income generated by the users' businesses.

Connecting families to technology is also an important outcome of CTC use at Washington CASH. For example, Sylvia shared that her 24-year-old son lacked computer literacy skills. She was proud that she "has been able to start explaining some computer stuff to him after taking the computer classes." This important step can foster digital inclusion among family members.

Community Benefits

Perhaps the most significant outcomes stemming from the use of Washington CASH's CTC are the ones associated with the community. Illustrating this point, the program coordinator indicated that the community thrives from having affordable, local, and responsible businesses in their midst. Although the organization has not conducted research into its long-term impact, the coordinator could offer a long list of successful Washington CASH businesses, providing examples such as a cleaning business that uses only organic detergents and a business that makes and sells chemical-free soaps. She went on to give the example of Leo's Plumbing, a successful Washington CASH protégé that now refers clients to other businesses started through the Washington CASH program.

Furthermore, Washington CASH builds community by working widely with other organizations, by providing and receiving referrals from low-income housing providers and the Urban League, among others. Most of their users are either referred from another organization or hear about Washington CASH via word of mouth.

Obstacles to Overcome

While overall Sylvia was pleased with the services offered at Washington CASH, she did point out that the center does not have all of the software she needs. She explained that they do not have the latest version of the Microsoft Windows operating system, Windows Vista. They also do not have the software application for Microsoft Access, which is a very useful program for keeping track of business records. Sylvia relayed that she was interested in learning how to run her business as a nonprofit, but Washington CASH only provided very basic information on how to go about it, so she had to find the information herself. In addition, Sylvia pointed out that there were a lot of different instructors coming and going, and the classes tended to be quite basic. She would like to see some classes spread out over a number of weeks or taught for longer durations on the weekends, to allow more time to go into subjects in depth.

Similarly, the coordinator spoke of certain limitations and obstacles that Washington CASH faces. The organization is currently limited to Kitsap, Pierce, and King counties; it would like to expand but lacks the funding. It also lacks funds to increase staffing, improve its facilities by updating desktop computers and laptops, and buy new software. The program coordinator gave the example of Photoshop, saying that it is currently only available on a limited number of computers.

Furthermore, the coordinator indicated that she would ideally like to upgrade the computer systems and software and then begin marketing the classes more aggressively; right now, she was afraid that if she marketed the classes, she would end up with too many students and not enough computers for them to use. She would also like to start offering online computer training tutorials. For all of these improvements, increased grant funding was highlighted as a key enabler. The coordinator also suggested that increased volunteer involvement would improve the computer center. She hoped to find an expert to volunteer in the center full-time to answer users' technical questions. As it currently stands, computer questions are typically answered by regular staff, which can interfere with their other duties.

Understanding the Impact

It is important to note that the primary aim of Washington CASH is to aid people in establishing small local businesses, rather than educating them about technology and increasing computer literacy. However, Washington CASH's services to potential small-business owners in the low-income bracket are clearly dependent upon computer technology and training. Although there are classes specifically introducing users to the basics of computers, the staff makes a concerted effort to incorporate computer skills into their other business classes.

Benefits for individual users are large. Users gain basic computer skills, including a variety of more advanced technology skills that are specifically tailored to launching and maintaining a successful business. According to the Washington CASH website (www.washington cash.org), since 1995 almost 1,300 low-income individuals have completed their business training courses, more than 600 businesses have either been launched or developed, and almost 300 loans have been granted totaling more than $600,000. Business owners from across the spectrum have availed themselves of the educational and support services offered through the organization. As its website proudly reports, "75 percent of our clients have experienced an increase in household income, and 56 percent report a significant increase in business revenue," after working with the organization.

This increase in business learning and household income can have positive effects on the families and communities of individual users. Families benefit from the extra money brought into the household and can pass on their new technology and business skills to family members. In turn, the communities benefit from having an increase in successful, sustainable small businesses and an increase in employment opportunities for local populations.

CHAPTER 10

Delridge Neighborhoods Development Association—Integrating Learning With Living

Meghan Madonna and Theresa Benson

Founded in 1996, the Delridge Neighborhoods Development Association (DNDA) identifies itself as a private nonprofit housing organization, based in the community of Delridge in West Seattle. The Delridge district of Seattle encompasses neighborhoods in a 10-square-mile area of the southwestern part of the city. City planning data, retrieved from the 2000 U.S. Census, reveals that 33,000 residents call this area home. Of this populace, approximately 25 percent are children. On its website (www.dnda.org), DNDA notes the following common characteristics of the neighborhoods that make up the Delridge district:

- Delridge Way is a major means of access to (and through) our community.
- Our ethnic and economic diversity is perhaps unrivaled throughout Seattle.
- We share a unique and varied geography of forested ridges and hillsides.
- We are part of the Longfellow Creek/Puget Creek Watershed.

DNDA's main purpose is to create a thriving Delridge community by bringing together neighbors, other nonprofits, businesses, and local government to build community, preserve affordable housing, enhance the natural environment, and provide opportunities for youth development through cultural arts programs.

Croft Place CTC

One of DNDA's affordable housing efforts is Croft Place Townhomes, an environmentally and community-friendly apartment complex that offers families in southwestern Seattle access to affordable and secure housing, human support services, and opportunities to build community. Croft Place features energy-efficient units, a centralized courtyard and play space, and a community technology center (CTC). The development is comprised of a diverse group of 21 households, and all families have incomes under 50 percent of the Seattle area median. Fifty children live in the complex, the majority of whom are elementary school age or younger. Fifteen households are headed by single parents, and seven apartments are reserved for families in transition out of homelessness. Families in the transitional units at Croft Place receive case management services for 2 years, at which time those services are transferred to another family in need. Families may stay as nontransitional tenants as long as they are able to afford to stay, and DNDA does everything within its means to ensure that housing is accessible to these families, whether it is at Croft Place or another housing location. Croft Place represents a diverse community that includes immigrants from Somalia, Ethiopia, Eritrea, and Cambodia. Approximately half of the families at Croft Place are African-American.

DNDA actively encourages community building, for example, through the provision of common areas for tenants. One of these common areas is the CTC, a computer lab that is open to tenants when a staff member or property manager is onsite to provide access. The center was incorporated into the design of the housing complex as a means of providing computer access to members of the Croft Place community. The center does not offer classes or specific programs, but rather it is an open lab for all residents to use. Due to damage done to the CTC from roughhousing, youth are currently required to be supervised while using the room and equipment.

The lab is a small room, about the size of a home office, housing three computers and a printer/scanner on an L-shaped desk. At the time of our visit, all computers were functioning properly. The computers run the Windows XP operating system, contain an array of software including the Microsoft Office Suite, and come equipped with high-speed internet access. There are three office chairs in the lab, two of which are in good condition and one with its back broken off. Inside the lab, there is a small bookshelf with binders providing information on community and social services. There is a large window with blinds drawn, and the room is clean and well lit. A case manager's office is connected to the CTC space.

A variety of community partnerships assists technology efforts and offerings at Croft Place. The organization works closely with NPower, a technology training and consulting agency for nonprofits. DNDA also works with One Economy to provide computers to residents of their housing developments. While the technology center at Croft Place can be categorized as small, conversations with staff and teenagers imply that the benefits to residents are large.

Interviewing at Croft

Researchers paid a visit to Croft Place Townhomes with a view to finding out more about the impact of the CTC on residents and the community. Two staff interviews were conducted at Croft Place: one with community builder Saeed, who has worked for the organization for 4 years, and the other with youth after-school supervisor and program manager Jamal, who is new to DNDA. A focus group was also conducted with teenage users. The researchers were also allowed to observe the technology center.

Reaching the Residents

Like many aspects of life, different values may be assigned to organizations and facilities by disparate people. For this reason, researchers wanted to learn why this CTC was important to its users, how they learned about it, as well as the frequency of their visits.

According to Jamal, a recent hire and youth supervisor, the CTC at Croft Place is an important resource to many users as "it's the only computer time that they get." Additionally, its proximity to users was highlighted as one reason for the CTC's success. Saeed, who works as DNDA's community builder, explained, "It's right here." Both staff members noted that the next closest place to use computers and the internet free of charge was the library, which is located more than a mile and a half away and is difficult to access without transportation or with children in tow. Typically the center is used for homework, job searches, locating resources online, and email.

In response to how often residents use the center, staff indicated that some of the core users stop by four times per week, whereas the average user comes in one time per week. Teenage participants Tom and Natalie said they had learned about the CTC from the program director and have been visiting regularly ever since. While both kids have a computer and dial-up internet access at home, they prefer to come to the lab because it has faster internet connectivity and software applications that they do not have at home, for example, Microsoft PowerPoint. Natalie stated that she uses the lab approximately every other day for up to 2 hours each day, while Tom uses it mostly during the school year for about 30 minutes each day.

Individual Benefits

The DNDA strives to provide opportunities for residents of the Delridge community through services such as the CTC at Croft Place. Both staff and focus group participants indicated that individual users of the CTC have experienced successes in a number of ways. For instance, children and teenagers were able to expand on their interests and hobbies, as well as use the facility for homework and research projects. In support of this outcome, Natalie reported that she uses the center to "do a lot of research," while both she and Tom rely on it for homework in general. Saeed confirmed that children come to the center throughout the year to work on homework assignments.

Computer and internet access at the CTC allow users to communicate with friends and family through email and social networking sites such as Facebook. While children preferred social networking and adults opted for email, remaining connected with friends, family, and community members is an important outcome for these residents.

Skill development speaks to another positive outcome of center use. Children at Croft Place have used the computers to create a resident newsletter and community music CDs. Adults have employed the computers to advertise upcoming community events. Saeed relays, "The CTC has helped a lot of people who thought they didn't know how to do anything; for example, one woman wanted to have a bake sale to raise money for community events. By using the CTC, she was able to learn to use Publisher and market the sale to other residents."

In this low-income community, jobs take on an important aspect in day-to-day living. For this reason, the impact of the CTC on employment is significant, as it allows users to write resumes, search for employment, and apply for jobs online. With so many employers requiring that job applications be submitted electronically, access to internet-capable technology can make the difference between getting hired and remaining unemployed.

Family Benefits

Families as well as individuals experience positive outcomes as a consequence of using the CTC at Croft Place. Given that one-third of the households in the building are transitional units, one of the most common uses of the CTC by adults was to look for permanent housing resources online. Saeed shared a compelling example:

> A year ago, the Section 8 (subsidized) housing waiting list opened for applications for a short period of time. This program, which provides sliding-scale housing vouchers for families based on income and circumstance, historically has a jam-packed wait list, and families often miss the opportunity to simply get on the list. Five families from Croft Place were able to apply online at the CTC, and four of those five were consequently chosen in the voucher lottery.

The provision of even more affordable housing allows families greater security in meeting their needs. While these families could have applied for the housing program in person, it is possible that other barriers (transportation, childcare, etc.) may have gotten in the way of going to the office to apply. In this case, the CTC had been a great help to people in securing affordable housing.

Safety is always a concern for parents, and the CTC provides a secure place for their children to socialize and work. Parental concern over what their kids were accessing online prompted parents to come together and, with the help of staff and volunteers, assemble a list of center rules to increase user safety. For example, no teenagers were allowed to be in the CTC without an adult present, and a list of questionable websites was compiled for filtering.

Community Benefits

In addition to expected community gains from access to technology and skill development, staff relayed that the CTC has brought people together to solve collective problems. One example was cited earlier, as residents came together to develop a set of rules for computer use at the center. In effect, the CTC acted as a catalyst for effective community involvement, a worthwhile outcome for any underserved community.

The CTC has promoted environmental stewardship in the Croft Place community, particularly among youth residents. One after-school project was centered around a nature scavenger hunt in the wetlands near the local elementary school. Staff and students used digital cameras to take photos of the local environment, which they uploaded and printed back at the CTC. Saeed noted that the youth "really got into it," as they simultaneously learned about nature, technology, and the community in which they live. This kind of educational project can have a positive impact on the community as youth develop a greater sense of pride and care for the environment in which they live.

Technical knowledge and skills gained at the CTC were also shared among residents, thus increasing digital inclusion at Croft Place. According to Saeed, "We have families who don't have any exposure to technology, and they learn through other residents." To fortify this assertion, Saeed provided the following examples: "Kids really love to burn CDs for an event or a party, and they enjoy showing others how to copy them. ... We have one resident who works at Wells Fargo [Bank]. That person gave a presentation to other residents on how to set up savings accounts and do online banking at the CTC." Teenage users Natalie and Tom indicated that they enjoyed passing on their technology knowledge to younger children in the lab and helping them learn such tasks as typing and searching the internet. This skill sharing benefits the community by helping members to expand available options to CTC use, whether it be for entertainment or financial purposes.

Moving Forward

While the opportunities provided by the CTC at Croft Place are abundant, some challenges also exist. For example, the number of computers is limited, and the CTC can only be accessed through staff members who have multiple duties both on and off site. Focus group youth affirmed this, saying that their primary barrier to using the lab was access. When the key holder is not on site, users must find the property manager to open the lab for them. They say they often cannot find him, which means they cannot always get into the lab when needed. These two participants suggested that, in addition to more access to the lab, having a person at the center to provide technology support would be beneficial to CTC users. Saeed noted that residents are sometimes unfamiliar with the tools and resources that are available to them, and this may result in a lack of use or sometimes misuse. Jamal emphasized that, "Kids are learning, and they need a lot of supervision and guidance." Croft Place staff agreed that financial resources for staffing the CTC or developing a formal volunteer program to staff the CTC at regular times, offering supervision, technology training and classes, and technical assistance, would help eliminate these barriers and create higher levels of access for all community residents.

Staff at Croft Place would also like to be able to develop programs to encourage more peer-to-peer information sharing as well as programs that benefit families holistically. Staff relayed that DNDA recently applied for a grant called "Families Connect" in order to offer a digital photography class to all families at all properties. This class intended to teach digital photography skills to families, offer a place for them to get to know one another and tell their stories, and then provide them with a digital camera of their own. Unfortunately, the foundation denied the grant because it would not provide expedient evidence of asset building such as job acquisition. Jamal sighed as he stated the following, "They didn't see the benefit of incentive and the value to community." Croft Place staff plan to keep the project in hand and look for other funders.

Digital Inclusion

The visit to the Croft Place CTC enabled insights to the many potential uses, successes, and challenges of CTCs. In the economically and ethnically diverse neighborhood of Delridge, supporting digital inclusion is a necessary element of building a strong community. At Croft Place, a program that provides housing and promotes community through participation, the CTC is a valuable resource to residents who do not have computers and printers or cannot afford internet service. It helps residents look for employment and housing and do schoolwork more efficiently and effectively. Residents have the opportunity to learn computer skills that build confidence and translate to valuable job skills. The CTC also brings people together to share information and solve problems. Adults have come together to create solutions, services, and products that lead to a stronger community. Teenagers help younger children use the computers, showing that the CTC can be a place for developing leadership skills as well as learning. Children utilize digital media as a means of expanding learning in other areas. Staff and residents at Croft Place recognized that the CTC would benefit from additional staff, however, as a lack of available staff to unlock the door as necessary, supervise youth, and provide computer assistance and instruction has been a barrier to use. Staff members are committed to removing these barriers by recruiting volunteers to supervise the CTC and accessing various funding sources to increase offerings that are beneficial and relevant to residents of Croft Place.

CHAPTER 11

Analyzing the Impacts

Carol F. Landry

As evidenced by the vibrant stories of the seven organizations we visited, community technology centers (CTCs) have a tremendous impact on the lives of the individuals who use them, their families, and their communities, increasing digital inclusion across Washington State. In order to better understand the vast wealth of information collected, we coded the composite impact of the CTCs according to six outcome categories: Employment and Economic Indicators, Academic Skills and Literacy, Social Inclusion and Personal Growth, Independence, Access to Information and Resources, and Communication. A full discussion of the creation of the outcome categories is included in Chapter 12, where we examine the underlying model that can be used to frame a discussion of these results with policymakers. We also consolidated the answers we received from users and staff in relation to the challenges facing these CTCs and the solutions they presented to overcome these challenges.

Understanding the Case Study Organizations

Across the seven organizations, 16 staff members and 38 users were interviewed, generating a rich data set for understanding how different organizations contribute to promoting digital inclusion across key population segments. Of the 16 staff members interviewed, 39 percent reported that they were employed for less than one year, 11 percent for 1–2 years, 22 percent for 3–5 years, and 28 percent for 6–10 years. Forty-seven percent of staff identified their role at the CTC as administrators or managers, and 47 percent reported that their role was as staff, for example, cook, cleaner, or monitor of the CTC; yet, only 7 percent of staff members self-identified as teachers.

Who Are the Users of Washington State CTCs?

When asked how users found out about their CTCs, the most reported information sources were friends or acquaintances, family members, and outreach from CTC staff. Less common were newspaper ads, peer agencies, or that the CTC was part of a larger agency. As shown in Table 11.1, approximately one-fifth of users had been coming to the center for 1 year or less, while just over 36 percent attended for 2 years, and 27 percent had used the center for 3 or more years. With almost two-thirds of users coming to the CTC for 2 or more years, it is clear that centers not only attract users to their programs, but they provide services that encourage users to return year after year.

Table 11.1 When Users Began to Come to the CTC

When Started	Users (n=33)
Less than one year ago	21.2%
1 year ago	15.2%
2 years ago	36.4%
3 years ago	12.1%
4 or more years ago	15.1%

We asked staff to identify the users who came to their centers. Youth and immigrants were identified most frequently, with residents, staff, low-income, and adult users also listed. This mirrors findings from the telephone survey (discussed in Chapter 3) that youth and immigrants were frequent users of the 47 centers who participated, again illustrating that CTCs are serving some of the most underserved populations in Washington State.

Additionally, the majority of users stated that the average amount of time spent at the center ranged from less than 1 hour up to 6 hours per week, but almost one-quarter used the center 7 or more hours per week (see Table 11.2). Supplementing user responses, staff suggested that the average length of time users visited the center was typically two to three times per week (54 percent), with 39 percent presenting 4 or more times, and 8 percent coming at least one time per week. These figures are significantly higher than the conservative estimate of 14 times per year given in Chapter 3, which was calculated using data from the telephone survey and from grantees of the Bill & Melinda Gates Foundation. The extent of CTC use bolsters the contention that these organizations are providing a valuable and much needed service in Washington State.

Table 11.2 Amount of Time Users Spend at CTCs Each Week

Case Studies	Users (n=21)
Less than 1–3 hours per week	23.8%
4–6 hours per week	38.1%
7–10 hours per week	9.5%
More than 10 hours per week	14.3%
Don't know—too irregular to determine	14.3%

Going beyond the question of CTC use, we looked at the reasons people came to the centers. With regard to computer and internet access, 75 percent of users said they had access at such places as the library, school, and home; however, those with home access noted that they had slower connections or dial-up connections, or lacked needed software on home equipment. Yet, fostering digital inclusion involves offering more than access to hardware and software, and this is evident from the stories of those interviewed at the case study sites. Staff reported that users sought information pertaining to jobs or center classes most often, while information about English, housing, entertainment, computer literacy, special interests such as music, and homework were wanted less frequently. According to users, English classes and digital technology were activities tried most often, followed by GED prep classes, presentation fundamentals, and email. Research, website design, basic computer classes, word processing, and business-related classes, on the other hand, were attempted less frequently.

CTC Benefits

The breadth of CTC benefits are visible on several levels: individual, family, and community. These benefits will now be reviewed with regard to the six outcomes outlined earlier.

Individual Benefits

Findings indicate that many benefits have been accrued for the individual user. Of the 235 answers given in response to the question of CTC impact, which allowed for multiple responses (see Table 11.3), 12 percent pointed to the Academic Skills and Literacy outcome, as centers helped users by providing references and/or resumes for college or jobs, facilitated academic improvement such as raising grades, and prepared users to obtain a GED or go to college. Demonstrating this outcome, La Casa Hogar's English as a Second Language (ESL) and GED preparation courses helped Latino immigrants develop English skills and attain GEDs in preparation for college. With regard to fiscal concerns, almost 23 percent of responses pointed to the Employment and Economic outcome. In this category, participants across the seven organizations specified that users acquired skills that prepared them for a job, empowered them to obtain additional technical skills, and helped them to gain employment.

By far, the greatest individual impact was noted for the Social Inclusion and Personal Growth outcome (36 percent). An assortment of characteristics such as relationship building and friendship, staying out of trouble, acquiring new interests or expanding existing interests, developing tangible skills (e.g., leadership, public speaking), and providing connections to community leaders were reported as significant benefits for individual users. However, the skills of building confidence and the ability to elevate expectations were found to be most significant, as involvement with these CTCs helped people to realize they were capable of doing more than they believed

Table 11.3 How Individuals Have Benefited from CTCs

Outcomes	Users
Academic Skills and Literacy	11.5%
Access to Information and Resources	10.2%
Employment and Economic	22.6%
Social Inclusion and Personal Growth	35.7%
Independence	7.9%
Other	1.3%

possible. For example, the Delridge Neighborhoods Development Association (DNDA) CTC helped people who were not familiar with technology overcome their fear and doubts that they could learn to use a computer. Similarly for the kids of Jefferson County 4-H Network News, media skill development increased their optimism and forward thinking as they began to see a future that extended beyond the poverty of their community.

The Access to Information and Resources outcome represented just over 10 percent of responses as users benefited from access to technology and used internet resources to pursue interests or look for work. Likewise, the Independence outcome recorded fewer than 10 percent of all replies for developing the ability to communicate in English, fill out and submit government forms online, and gain the ability to drive oneself. Finally, the Other outcome includes the benefit of a safe and comfortable environment, whereas having free or low-cost access to the CTC was found to be less significant.

Family Benefits

Looking more broadly for impact, we explored how users' families benefited from their use of CTCs, which can be seen in Table 11.4. Of the 50 responses about family benefits, staff and users indicated that the greatest gain pertained to the Academic Skills and Literacy outcome (40 percent), and of these, the majority referred to the benefit of connecting families to technology. Examples include a teen assisting

Table 11.4 How Families Have Benefited from CTCs

Outcomes	Users
Academic Skills and Literacy	40.0%
Communication	18.0%
Employment and Economic	12.0%
Social Inclusion and Personal Growth	22.0%
Other	8.0%

his father to order items online and a mom explaining computer technology to her son. An equally important but less frequent response for the family was the ability to help school-age children. Being both parents and users, adults found that it was beneficial to use the CTC to assist their kids with homework and research projects. This support, in turn, helped children do better in school.

Under the Social Inclusion and Personal outcome, 22 percent of replies applied to improving family relationships and keeping kids safe by checking their online activities. Reel Grrls facilitated family relations by supporting girls who wished to tell their stories through movies. Such accounts helped to restore fractured relationships as girls voiced their concerns and struggles in a video format. Regarding online safety, by learning how to use computers, parents were able to track kids' online activities, for example, by checking to see if they were looking for information on guns or pornography.

CTCs further benefited families by keeping them connected, as evidenced by the 18 percent of responses attributed to the Communication outcome. This is all the more significant as many users are immigrants, and CTCs allow them to stay in touch with family members abroad, for example, in Mexico where there are many cybercafés. In terms of the Employment and Economic outcome, 12 percent of replies credited CTCs for helping users get a better paying job, and higher income employment benefited families by making it easier to meet day-to-day expenses. Finally, 8 percent of responses applied to the Other outcome for such worthwhile benefits as obtaining more affordable housing for the family as a consequence of filling out and submitting application forms online.

Community Benefits

Of the 76 responses pertaining to community impact, participants indicated that the Employment and Economic outcome was the most significant to users' communities, with 42 percent of responses being attributed to a more highly skilled work force and to a better educated population (see Table 11.5). For example, at La Casa Hogar, all current staff had risen from the ranks of students into leadership positions at the center as a consequence of CTC training. At Tacoma Clubhouse, CTC offerings have resulted in a large portion of its at-risk teenage population going on to college, securing internships, or obtaining quality jobs.

Table 11.5 How Communities Have Benefited from CTCs

Outcomes	Users
Employment and Economic	42.1%
Independence	14.5%
Social Inclusion and Personal Growth	34.2%
Other	9.2%

CTC impact was soundly represented in the Social Inclusion and Personal Growth outcome. Just over 34 percent of responses revealed that the community benefited from CTCs in helping to develop future leaders, and due to the community building aspect of the center, users are motivated to take action in their communities. DNDA users shared their skills as they helped others to learn CTC technology, while La Casa Hogar's support of immigrants made it possible for those who knew more to teach those who knew less. 4-H Network News challenges kids to be more than a cog in the wheel of bureaucracy, while La Casa Hogar helped to empower women to become leaders in their neighborhoods. In addition, it was found that all of the CTCs targeting youth in their programs are contributing toward creating a safer community, providing youth with a positive space to hang out and learn.

Lastly, the Independence outcome associated with community is the ability to speak and be understood without the need for a translator. Although more important to immigrants than other CTC users, such independence lessens the demands on community resources as fewer translators are required for medical, government, and legal interactions.

Challenges to Using CTCs

Of the 55 responses addressing challenges to using either the CTC or its technologies, almost 22 percent dealt with insufficient space, computers, or technologies (see Table 11.6). The overwhelming concern was the lack of space and computers. By having an insufficient number of computers, frustrated users were forced to wait for a unit to become available or were dissuaded from using the center altogether. Independent of the center, school or work demands interfered with CTC use. Other less common but important dilemmas faced by users included transportation, lack of training or basic skills to use technology, insufficient levels of staffing, lack of time, language barriers, lack of computer and internet, intimidation of technology, and childcare issues. These findings are consistent with the answers of staff in the telephone survey discussed in Chapter 3. Although users and staff had different perspectives on which were more important, we found many commonalities among most of the barriers identified by both groups.

Hindrances to Future Development

When asked about problems regarding future program development at CTCs, 24 percent of 29 responses were directed at inadequate staffing or teachers, and 24 percent targeted funding issues, as shown in Table 11.7. Too little staffing was tied to myriad issues, from lacking qualified teachers for classroom instruction to limiting the hours a center was open. Staffing was frequently viewed as a key component to future development. Funding also presented a significant obstacle for centers, since such concerns affected many aspects of the CTCs. Without sufficient funding, additional staff could not be hired and updates to equipment and software were put on hold, along with

Table 11.6 Challenges to Using CTCs or Technology

Challenges	Users
Childcare	3.6%
Intimidation of technology	9.1%
Insufficient space/ computers/technology	21.8%
Insufficient staff/teachers	5.5%
Lack of access away from CTC	7.3%
Lack of training/basic skills	9.1%
Language	9.1%
Not enough time	7.3%
Transportation	7.3%
Work/school commitments	12.7%
Other	7.3%

purchasing new computers and applications. Additionally, participants pointed to a lack of space, insufficient time, and users' unfamiliarity with hardware or software as hindrances to CTCs future development.

Needed for Future Improvement

Of the 99 responses, the greatest need pertained to increased training, classes, and programming (see Table 11.8). For some, expanded classes in ESL would be the direction; for others, more in-depth technology classes were needed. Echoing the challenges that users faced and hindrances experienced by CTCs, future hopes for improvement included the addition of more staff, more and better resources, more

Table 11.7 Hindrances to CTCs' Future Developments

Hindrances	Staff/Users
Funding	24.1%
Inadequate staffing/teachers	24.1%
Lack of resources (computer/software)	13.8%
Lack of space	6.9%
Lack of time	10.3%
Users' unfamiliarity with hardware/software	10.3%
Other	10.3%

space, and increased funding. Additional staff would permit CTCs to remain open for longer hours or allow an expansion of class offerings. More space would mean larger classrooms that could be equipped with additional computers. Increased funding could address a host of issues facing CTCs. With it, concern over sustainability would be reduced and the problems centered on the issues of space, classes, resources, and staff would be decreased. To a lesser degree, more outreach, increased hours of operation, additional community partnerships, childcare, and other factors were also considered important for future improvement.

A number of the CTCs we visited felt that their organization needed to expand to keep centers relevant to the needs of the Washington State community. Tacoma Clubhouse would like to develop into a series of campuses, each dedicated to a specific program. Washington CASH was limited to Kitsap, Pierce, and King counties, but it would like to be a presence in other counties as well. Similarly, Reel Grrls would like to take the program on the road, within Washington State and beyond.

Conclusion

Washington State CTCs play an important role in bringing positive benefits to users, their families, and their communities. They are significant

Table 11.8 Needs for Future Improvement of CTCs

Improvement	Staff/Users
Childcare	3.0%
More/better resources (software/hardware)	14.1%
More community partnerships	5.1%
More funding	11.1%
More outreach	6.1%
More space	11.1%
More staff/teachers	15.2%
More time/hours	8.1%
More training/classes/expanded programming	21.2%
Other	5.1%

for providing underserved populations with the type of digital inclusion opportunities enjoyed by more privileged members of these communities. Users can become more informed, better educated, and independent members of society, and this betterment is a gain to Washington State as people require less state support. Yet, as will be discussed fully in Chapter 12, despite their triumphs, CTCs struggle to articulate to funders in a way that highlights the importance of their work to broader policy issues.

Part 3

A Framework for Measurement

CHAPTER 12

The Situated Logic Model: A Method for Measuring Impact

Charles M. Naumer

Community technology centers (CTCs) are unique in that the work they do is often critically important to the work of other community efforts and broad policy initiatives. Programs delivering social services related to policy issues such as workforce development, public health, and education may rely on technology for purposes of 1) administering programs including registering online for services, 2) communicating through email and websites, and 3) delivering services such as online training or access to information. Without access to technology and the skills to use it, many members of the targeted populations will not be able to avail themselves of these services.

The challenge confronting CTCs is how to frame and communicate their work in a way that will be of interest to policymakers and be relevant to the funding streams that come from policy decisions. This chapter discusses the difficulties involved in making the work of CTCs relevant to policymakers and explains the steps that the University of Washington research team took to derive a solution to this challenge. The strengths and weaknesses of the logic model, one of the most commonly used methods for assessing impact, are discussed. Finally, a modification of the logic model, in the form of the Situated Logic Model, is presented as a means of better measuring the impact of CTCs on the *whole* communities they serve. In Chapter 13, a step-by-step process for using the Situated Logic Model to evaluate the work of CTCs in a more holistic manner is introduced.

Opportunities and Challenges of Measuring Impact

The role of CTCs in a community is often one of support to larger initiatives. For example, La Casa Hogar's outcomes included increased confidence in using computers, better job prospects, increased community participation, greater ability to support children's education, and improved personal educational attainment and English skills. From a policy perspective, the work of La Casa Hogar has implications for issues related to the integration of nonnative speakers into communities, workforce development, the economy, and education. Programs engaged in areas such as workforce development, public health, and education all benefit from the work conducted by La Casa Hogar.

The challenge confronting CTCs such as La Casa Hogar is communicating the connection between these efforts and their work. As will be explained, our work showed that CTCs impact important policy issues such as employment and economic, academic skills and literacy, social inclusion and personal growth, independence, access to information and resources, and communication. However, CTC staff may have difficulties understanding the larger policy contexts in which their work plays a role, not the least because the social environments in which CTCs operate are complex and dynamic. Staying abreast of policy issues in a community and being able to establish linkages between the work of the CTC and those policy issues, requires considerable time and effort.

This problem may also be exacerbated by the lack of tools and approaches available to establish these broader linkages. As will be discussed in detail later in the chapter, logic models are narrow and linear in focus, and fail to capture the work of a CTC in the context of larger policy issues. These models also lack the ability to assess impact beyond the confines of the work being done in the CTC, isolating the work of a CTC within the confines of the programs delivered.

These challenges reflect the need to better frame the work of CTCs in a policy context and the need to create methodologies that provide CTCs with better tools for understanding and reporting their impact. One of the key elements of making the connection between the work of CTCs and relevant policy issues is the actual act of defining the policy issue itself. Once the issue has been identified, understanding the relevance of the CTCs work to that issue becomes much easier.

Survey of Existing Indicator Sets

To understand the larger policy issues relevant to the work of CTCs, our team conducted an extensive review of the relevant literature surveying the landscape for indicators to measure community impact. These indicators were collected, collated, and grouped into six major categories: Employment and Economic Indicators, Academic Skills and Literacy, Social Inclusion and Personal Growth, Independence, Access to Information and Resources, and Communication. These indicator sets are represented in the left column of Table 12.1.

The next step was to see if these indicators could be applied to existing studies and what, if any, evaluation mechanisms were currently being used. The indicators were mapped against those being used by nine agencies in Washington State: Casey Family Programs; Bill & Melinda Gates Foundation Community Access to Technology program; MGS Consulting; YWCA Working Zone; Microsoft Unlimited Potential program; City of Seattle Community Technology Program; United Way/WIN 211; Workforce Development Council of Seattle-King County; and Youth Force. Their use of the indicators is demonstrated in Table 12.1.[1] Most of the agencies were collecting at least some indicator information from one or more of the six categories. Only the last two categories, Access to Information and Resources and Communication, were not being measured in these particular situations.

Survey of Outcome Measures

Next, the research team surveyed the literature to assess best practices related to evaluating the impact of CTCs. By developing this broad set of impact measures, the team encountered many of the same challenges facing CTCs in defining impact. Many of the papers reviewed focused on the role of CTCs in a particular context. For example, we came across CTCs that assessed their impact in relation to digital inclusion, workforce training, and skills building. However, best practices for evaluating the impact of CTCs from a more holistic, policy-oriented perspective were limited.

We also surveyed the literature relating to the six policy areas. We found that the literature regarding these policy areas was much richer in terms of identifying and understanding outcome measures. Considerable work across multiple disciplines had been invested in understanding the processes impacting the policy issues identified.

Table 12.1 Indicators Used by Selected Agencies Interested in Social Impact Measures

Indicator \ Program	Casey Family Programs	Gates Foundation CAT Programs	MGS Consulting (CAT Grantee evaluation)	YWCA Working Zone	Microsoft Unlimited Potential	City of Seattle Community Technology Program	United Way/Win211	WorkForce Development Council of Seattle/King County	Youth Force (TechJobs.org)
Outcomes									
Employment / Economic									
Career planning skills	X	X		X	X				X
Learn software programs for job skill development									
Learn how to write a resume									
Housing/Money management skills	X	X		X					
Work life skills	X	X		X		X			X
Academic skills and literacy									
Improve school performance, grades			X						
Learn to speak and write in English									
Educational attainment		X	X			X			
Language skills		X				X			
Technology skills						X			
Information literacy skills		X							
Computer basics									
Database fundamentals									
Presentation fundamentals									
Wordprocessing fundamentals									
Social Inclusion and personal growth									
Social relationship skills	X	X	X		X	X			X
Gain confidence in one's ability to learn									
Connect and take action in one's community									
Constructive engagement with others			X						
Civic engagement			X						
Ethical behavior			X						
Independence									
Self care skills	X	X	X						
Change in self-sufficiency standard								X	
Gain economic independence - find an affordable place to live									
Learn adaptive technology to enable physical independence									
Daily living skills	X		X			X			
Access to Information and resources									
Find jobs and housing using the Internet									
Find services and resources using the Internet									
Communication									
Remain in contact with family (long distance) using e-mail									
Be active in local community associations and organizations using e-mail and the Internet									

This research base provided a strong basis for tying outcomes to impact. Specific outcome measures such as the acquisition of a skill were linked to the impact objective of the policy issue being addressed. These relationships were examined by mapping the policy issues and relevant stakeholders of the context in which a CTC is embedded to the processes of the CTC itself to visually depict the interrelationships. These visual representations provided the basis for developing more detailed logic models of the processes and establishing linkages to the work of CTCs.

As we examined the research regarding these six policy areas using the techniques discussed, we began to better understand the role of

CTCs' work in facilitating the processes leading to impact. We began to see strong supportive relationships between the work of CTCs and the actions and outcomes leading to social impact identified in the literature. As a result, we began to conceptualize the outcome measures for CTCs in terms of their relationship to the actions and outcome measures identified in the research regarding the identified policy issues.

Survey and Case Studies

Following our efforts to assess existing outcome measurement approaches from the literature, we turned to gathering information from Washington State CTCs regarding their practices of measuring outcomes. Through the survey and case study analysis, we found that many of the CTCs were using evaluation approaches that employed the use of logic models to describe impact. These efforts were largely disconnected from the larger policy issues affecting their communities, instead focusing their efforts on measuring and reporting outcomes of only their target population. As a result, we noticed a disconnect between the outcome measures associated with the policy issues discussed in the literature and the outcome measures identified by the CTCs studied.

The Logic Model Considered

In many ways, logic models have become the lingua franca of the evaluation community. As a result of their widespread adoption and acceptance within both evaluation and policymaking communities, the use of logic models is an important topic to consider when developing an approach to measuring and reporting impact.

Patton (2002) describes a logic model as a framework for understanding what an organization does, how it does it, and what results. As depicted in Figure 12.1, this type of model is usually represented visually as a linear process that shows a linkage between program inputs, activities, processes, outputs, outcomes, and impact. Logic models provide a clear way for describing the participants and activities of a program as they relate to outcomes over time. These models are often used to help programs develop metrics or outcomes that they can report to organizations and other stakeholders, including policymakers.

Figure 12.1 Program Logic Model

A criticism of the logical framework analysis method is that it is highly reductive and linear, breaking down the work of programs into independent variables—for example, inputs, activities, and outputs—and only explaining the relationships between these variables. More importantly, from a systems perspective, this approach is limited in its ability to recognize the role of an organization or program within the context of larger systems. These limitations are as follows:

1. Tends to be highly linear explaining change as occurring according to a chain of events.
2. Focuses on independent variables.
3. Is reductive, reducing the work of a program to individual inputs and discrete activities, and expressing outcomes as single measures.
4. Is often program- or organization-centric, focused narrowly on the activities and impacts an organization has on its direct stakeholders.
5. Is static and unable to recognize the dynamic nature of factors associated with a program.
6. Tends to be relatively simplistic and unable to represent the complexity of the social systems in which it plays a role.

Based on CTCs' embeddedness in other efforts and their focus on building fundamental building blocks essential to the success of individuals in other programs, a systems approach to understanding CTC impact may be especially important. The necessity to frame their work using a more holistic perspective may make the weaknesses of logic models particularly problematic. Despite these weaknesses, our research team recognized the value of the widespread adoption of logic models. Our task became one of utilizing the model within a more holistic framework so that it might better reflect systemic changes as a measure of the impact of a CTC. The resulting model developed from this work, discussed here, is the Situated Logic Model.

The Situated Logic Model

This model, coined the Situated Logic Model, reflects the fact that the work of CTCs needs to be understood within the context of the larger policy issues it affects. In other words, the work of CTCs is situated within a larger context, and understanding the way that a CTC's work is situated is key to understanding impact in a context outside of individual programs. This model recognizes the fact that community technology is often embedded in other programs and processes. By using the Situated Logic Model approach, a CTC may assess, quantify, and represent its impact in the context of broader policy issues. In other words, the Situated Logic Model approach bridges the work of CTCs to broad policy areas.

For example, as demonstrated in Figure 12.2, linkages between a workforce development policy logic model and a CTC program logic model demonstrate the role that a CTC plays in supporting or enabling a workforce development program. The logic model representing workforce development was developed and supported by the

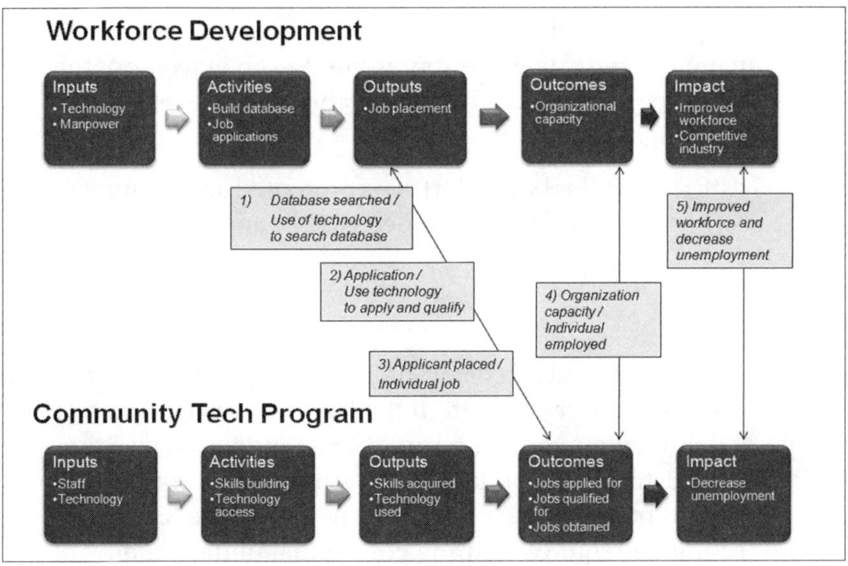

Figure 12.2 Situated Logic Model (Workforce Development)

literature documenting "common" and "best practices" regarding workforce development.

The logic model shown depicts a workforce development effort that facilitates the placement of displaced workers through the development and implementation of an online jobs database and application process. The workforce development model identifies the availability of a database listing job opportunities and a process for placing workers as a key strategy for redeploying displaced workers. This database is made available to job training programs and individuals seeking work. Figure 12.2 demonstrates how the work of CTCs enables the efforts of the workforce development effort as follows:

1. The first linkage demonstrates that an *output* of the workforce development model is the searching of the database. This *output* is made possible by the CTC program *outcome* of providing access and skills necessary for individuals needing to access online databases.
2. Similarly, the application for a job by a person is an *output* of the workforce development program and an *outcome* of the CTC program.
3. The placement of an individual in a job represents an *outcome* of the CTC program model and an *output* of the workforce development program.
4. The placement of an individual improves the capacity of an organization, which is represented as an *outcome* of the workforce development program and is an *outcome* of the CTC program.
5. Lastly, impact for both efforts is represented as an improvement of the workforce and a decrease in unemployment.

Conclusion

As demonstrated, the Situated Logic Model provides CTCs with a way of representing their impact within the larger context of the systems within which they operate. The use of logic models allows them to build upon existing work while using common methods used by policymakers and other decision makers. The use of the Situated Logic Model technique requires a strong conceptual understanding of the community and how CTC programs might support the work of the community. This chapter introduced the concept of a Situated Logic Model, and the next chapter will demonstrate a process that may be used to construct the Situated Logic Model in a larger process for assessing impact.

Endnote

1. The following are data sources for the columns in Table 12.1: MGS Consulting (for Bill & Melinda Gates Foundation CAT grants) (see www.mgs-us.com/OurClients/CAT_Final_Eval.pdf for source information); RECA Foundation (www.recafoundation.org) source information from personal email; Center for Internet & Society (www.cis.washington.edu) source information from personal email; YWCA Working Zone (www.ywcaworks.org/page/138) source information from personal email; Center to Bridge the Digital Divide (www.communitiesconnect.org) for Communities Connect Grantees; City of Seattle Community Technology Program (www.seattle.gov/tech/indicators); United Way/WIN211 (www.win211.org); Workforce Development Council of Seattle-King County (primary source at www.sixstrategies.org/files/WAcomplete.pdf; online version at www.seakingwdc.org/Templates/js_calculator.html); Casey Family Programs (www.caseylifeskills.org/pages/assess/assess_aclsa.htm); Youth Force (www.teenjobs.org); Program Logic Model (www.youthforce.com/ YFdocs.html).

CHAPTER 13

The Process: Putting It All Together

Charles M. Naumer

Introducing the Process

This chapter introduces a process that you can use to develop a Situated Logic Model as part of an iterative process directed at measuring and reporting the impact of your organization. The process has been designed to help community technology centers (CTCs) better understand and report their contributions in terms of the issues important to policymakers and funders. This process is composed of nine steps related to the following four larger stages (see Figure 13.1):

1. Understanding context
2. Developing a Situated Logic Model
3. Reporting outcomes
4. Reflecting on the process and models developed

The first set of steps in the process, Context Mapping, involves the mapping of the whole context in which the CTC is operating. This set of steps is implemented by identifying and defining the policy issues and stakeholder organizations with which the CTC intersects. The second stage of the process is focused on the development of the Situated Logic Model. This set of steps involves the logical mapping of an organization's outcomes in terms of the processes, policies, and systems within the context they are working. Thus, the analysis becomes grounded in the terminology that is commonly understood in describing the work of nonprofit and social sector organizations. The third stage in the process, Outcome Measurement, involves the identification and reporting of the most relevant outcomes. The last

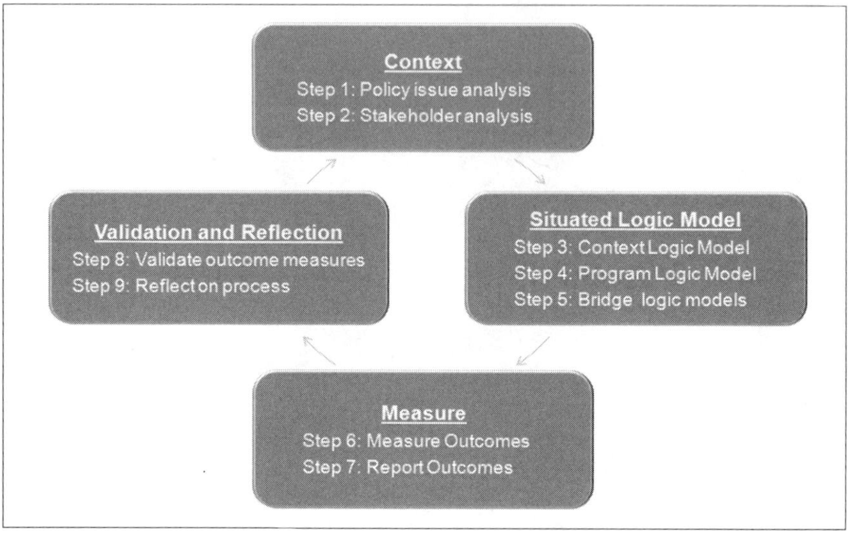

Figure 13.1 Community Technology Impact Measurement Process Model

set of steps, Validation and Reflection, requires an organization to challenge and validate this process and to use the Situated Logic Model to inspire and shape future work at the organization. The rest of this chapter gives a more detailed description of each step in the process.

Context Mapping

The context of your organization's work may be defined in terms of 1) policy issues and 2) the stakeholders associated with those policy issues. As stated previously, policy issues often associated with the work of CTCs include increased education, reduction of poverty, improved quality of life, increased civic engagement, and other widely accepted objectives for a healthy society. These are often defined very broadly at a macro level.

Step 1: Analyzing the Policy Issues

Analyzing policy issues requires you to identify the major issues confronting the community in which your CTC works. You should then highlight the policy areas that your organization impacts. This may require you to step back from the day-to-day realities of running a CTC in order to better understand the work of the CTC in a larger context. Worksheet 1 presents a series of questions that staff at your organization might ask to gain this broader perspective and to begin the process of better understanding and representing the role of your organization in the efforts of the larger community. The worksheet has been designed so that the collection and analysis of data will support the development of a Situated Logic Model. By addressing each of the questions listed on the worksheet, you should be able to identify the policy issues that your work impacts and begin to understand ways in which such work may be represented as impacting these issues.

Worksheet 1: Policy Issue Mapping

A policy issue mapping exercise is used to identify the major issues facing your community. Sources of information to address the following questions may include CTC staff, CTC clients, community members, news media articles, professional literature, and academic literature.

1. What are important policy issues facing your community? These policy issues might include general topic areas such as education, crime, housing, civic engagement, employment, and financial sustainability.

2. What are some of the concerns facing your clients? How are the efforts of the CTC impacting their objectives?

3. Who are the individuals, groups, and organizations addressing these policy issues in your community?

4. What are some of the important processes used to address these issues (for example, improved education is addressed by classroom instruction, access to technology, etc.)?

5. What are some of the important outcomes associated with these processes (for example, improved test scores, higher graduation rates, higher college enrollments, etc.)?

Policy Issue	Organizations	Processes	Outcomes
Education	• Schools • Online training organizations • Libraries	• Classroom instruction • Self-study	• Improved test scores • Graduation rates
Employment	• Workforce development agencies • Employers	• Job training • Job banks • Skill identification	• Lower unemployment rates • Workforce productivity measures
Housing	• Financial institutions • Individuals	• Housing assistance programs • Financial assistance	• Reduced homelessness • Asset building

Step 2: Analyzing the Stakeholders

You can begin to identify stakeholders: the individuals, groups, organizations, and institutions that affect the outcomes associated with the policy issues identified in Step 1. It is important to consider stakeholders as part of the larger processes associated with achieving the policy outcomes and not only as organizations that have a relationship with your CTC. A CTC's work may affect an organization with which it has neither a formal nor informal relationship.

You may then collect data about the actions, perceptions, behaviors, experiences, and thoughts of the stakeholders in relation to the services offered by their organization. Worksheet 2 has been designed to support the collection and analysis of this information. The questions presented in the worksheet provide a way to develop another level of detail regarding the work being accomplished and the approaches being taken in the community to address the identified policy issues. By developing a better understanding of the roles of stakeholders, your

CTC should be better able to understand its contribution to addressing the broader policy issues affecting the community. This process is based on stakeholder analysis as described by Burgoyne (1994).

Worksheet 2: Stakeholder Analysis

A stakeholder analysis involves identifying stakeholders, their intentions and desires, the processes they engage in, and finally their achieved outcomes. Sources of information to address the following questions may include CTC staff, CTC clients, community members, news media articles, professional literature, and academic literature.

1. Based on the policy issue mapping exercise, who are the major stakeholders regarding the identified policy issues?

2. What are important policy issues facing your community? (These policy issues might include general topic areas such as education, crime, housing, civic engagement, employment, and financial sustainability).

3. Who are the individuals, groups, and organizations addressing these policy issues in your community?

4. What are some of the important processes used to address these issues (for example, improved education is addressed by classroom instruction, access to technology, etc.)?

5. What are some of the important outcomes associated with these processes (for example, improved test scores, higher graduation rates, higher college enrollments, etc.)?

Stakeholder	Processes	Outcomes
K–12 Schools	• Classroom instruction • Online curricula	• Improved student achievement • Attendance
Employment	• Classroom • Learning tools • Online research	• Skills acquisition • Graduation
Workforce Development Programs	• Training programs • Build job databases • Collaborate with industry	• Place workers • Help workers develop new skills • Information provided to community regarding job opportunities

The Situated Logic Model

As demonstrated in Chapter 12, the Situated Logic Model approach allows an organization to describe its work within the context of the policy issues or stakeholder's work identified. The challenges of using a Situated Logic Model approach are to represent efforts in the community that address a policy issue and to link the work of your CTC to those efforts. The knowledge of the community that you have gained from carrying out Steps 1 and 2 can now be mapped out in the logic models in the following steps.

Step 3: Developing a Logic Model for Context

Based on the data collected and analysis performed in the context defining steps, you can now represent your understanding of the issue in terms of a logic model. You could either choose to create a logic model that maps out the context of multiple policy issues, or you could choose to focus on just one policy issue. For each policy issue, you should work to identify the following components of the logic model:

- Inputs – Including stakeholders, funding, and facilities
- Activities – Training, resource provision, and other actions taken to address the policy issue
- Outputs – Skills developed, jobs applied for, housing provided
- Outcomes – Placement of workers in jobs, provision of housing, and other outcomes reflecting the result of the work
- Impact – Larger benefits to society such as higher employment rates, reduction in homelessness, and better workforce

The resulting logic model should serve as a clear representation of the work being accomplished in the greater community around the identified policy issue.

Step 4: Developing a Logic Model for Your Program

The next step you should take in constructing the Situated Logic Model is to map out the logic of *your* organization's work in terms of the policy issue. This logic model should be developed based on an understanding of the processes that define your work. As in Step 3, you should include the inputs, activities, outputs, outcomes, and impacts of your CTC in relation to the policy issue.

Step 5: Bridging the Logic Models

Once you have developed a logic model for the context of the policy issue and a logic model for your CTC's intersection with that issue, the next step is to bridge the two models. This provides you with an easy way to visually map out the linkages between the work of your program and the work associated with the policy issue. For example, if one of your program outcomes is the acquisition of a skill and that skill is instrumental to accomplishing a specific task as defined in the context model, a linkage may be identified. This linkage shows that the development of a certain skill at your CTC is critical to the advancement of the work being accomplished at the policy level. Another example of a linkage might be if a citywide policy program directed at improving early childhood services disseminated information via a website, and the CTC facilitated that activity at the policy level by providing clients with the skills to use the internet and the technology to access the website. You can identify and highlight that linkage using the Situated Logic Model approach.

Outcome Measurement

Once the Situated Logic Model has been constructed, you will be ready to identify the outcome measures and report those measures to the public. As discussed, the linkages identified should be used to support arguments regarding the importance and relevance of the work of your CTC.

Step 6: Measuring the Outcomes

You can now identify the most important outcomes to measure, based on the linkages established between the context logic model and your program logic model. This will ensure that your outcome measures are grounded within the logic that ties your organization's outcomes to the processes of the broader policy issue. Using the example described earlier, a CTC could measure the outcomes associated with accessing the early childhood website by tracking the number of times clients accessed this website through usage tracking software and by tracking the skills used by parents to access the information resources by the use of a skills inventory and usage instrument or observation by CTC staff.

Step 7: Reporting the Outcomes

You can report the outcome measures using the Situated Logic Model (Figure 13.2). This model allows you to easily describe to funders and policymakers the relationship between your program's outcome measures and the processes and objectives associated with the policy context in which your program is embedded. Reporting outcomes by this method establishes the relevancy of your program to important policy issues in your community and provides a powerful visual aid for communicating the results of your work.

Validation and Reflective Practices

The last set of steps suggests that you reflect upon the entire process of evaluation described here, consider the ability of the outcome

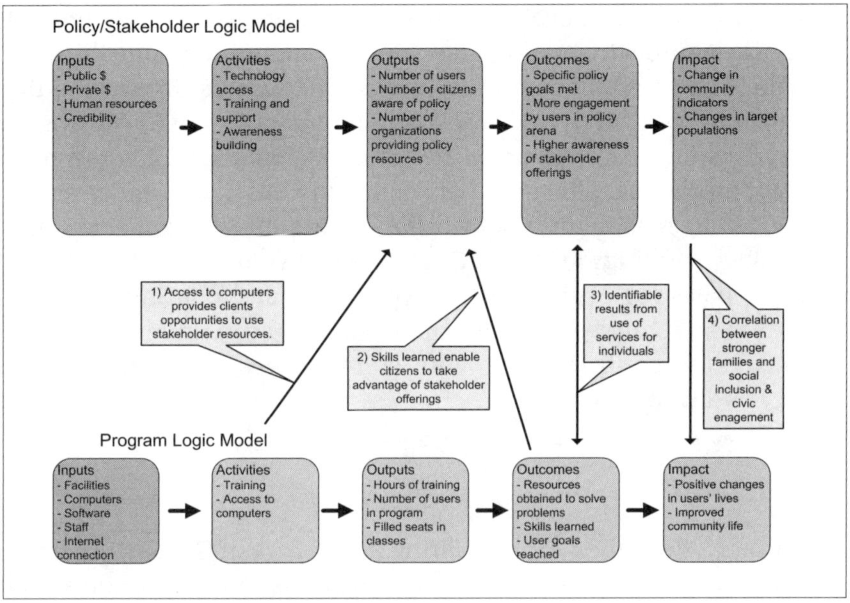

Figure 13.2 Situated Logic Model

measures to achieve the desired process and use the results of the Situated Logic Model to inform future work at your organization.

Step 8: Validating the Outcome Measures

Once your outcome measures have been defined, measured, and reported, you may validate them by re-examining their relationship to the larger context of the policy issue. Validation may entail interviewing stakeholders, engaging in dialogue with staff, interviewing CTC users, and performing other activities directed at challenging the validity of the assumptions you constructed in the Situated Logic Model. Given the dynamic nature of both the community environment in which a CTC operates and changes within the program, continual validation of outcome measures is important. The validation of outcome measures provides an important means for staff members to continually reflect on the validity of their efforts and improve their measures.

Step 9: Reflecting on Performance

Outcome measures are often used solely for summative and reporting purposes. It is important that your outcome measures are also used to inform and develop your organization's work. This type of formative approach should allow you to evaluate the contributions you are making to the community, examine ways of improving the effectiveness of your organization, and identify ways of improving as an organization. For example, the Situated Logic Model could help you to visualize new linkages between your CTC and broader policy issues, linkages that you might use to figure out how to expand the technology offerings at the CTC. This reflective process should provide the basis for beginning the cycle anew and continuing to re-envision and rebuild the framework so that you can understand your organization's contribution to the communities you serve and to society as a whole.

Conclusion

The process described for measuring the impact of CTCs is designed to assist community technology organizations to better understand and define their contributions in the context of policy issues important to the communities in which they work. This process is intended as a way to continually define and redefine the CTC's role in the community and to adapt toward a constantly changing landscape. By following this process, we believe that CTCs' value may be better recognized and that their contributions to their community and society as a whole will continue to develop.

References

Burgoyne, J. G. (1994). Stakeholder analysis. In C. Cassell & G. Symon (Eds.), *Qualitative methods in organizational research: A practical guide* (pp. 187–207). New Delhi: Sage.

CHAPTER 14

The Situated Logic Model in the Real World

Charles M. Naumer

In order to illustrate the development of a Situated Logic Model using the process described in Chapter 13, this chapter describes a real-world scenario for developing a Situated Logic Model by measuring the outcomes of a fictitious community technology center (CTC), called the EDGE. The EDGE CTC comprises a composite of characteristics of the organizations profiled in the case studies. Each of the nine steps of the approach will be discussed in detail, providing examples of how an organization could follow the approach and report impact in a way that is relevant to the issues of the community in which they work. This chapter employs techniques of persona and scenario development to illustrate the Community Technology Impact Measurement Process Model approach.

The EDGE CTC

The EDGE CTC is located in a high-poverty urban setting of the fictional city of Edgeville. The EDGE is named for its work to provide citizens of Edgeville with opportunities to access technology and develop important technology skills. The demographics of its clients are primarily adults between the ages of 18 and 65, the majority of whom are seeking employment. The EDGE received funding for its programs and has a dedicated, well-trained staff and a computer lab where they can deliver training. The EDGE offers open lab time along with technology training in the following programs: Windows for

Beginners, Word Processing for Beginners, Using the Internet, Using Email, Internet and Employment Research, and Resume Writing.

The EDGE works in a community with myriad important policy issues of great concern to its citizens, for example, education, reduction of poverty, quality of life, and civic engagement. The EDGE has often struggled to communicate to policymakers and funders that its work matters. The staff of the EDGE has found that many funders and policymakers are focused on these broader policy issues and often fail to see that the work of the EDGE can, and does, provide solutions to these problems. The situation is further complicated by the fact that policy issues are multifaceted and abstractly defined, making it difficult for the EDGE to clearly demonstrate the impact that its programs can have on these broader issues. The EDGE has struggled with the many different factors that contribute to achieving the larger outcomes, and it is difficult to isolate the role or contribution of a single factor within the complex processes that determine these outcomes. In short, the EDGE realizes that its work is foundational to other community efforts and needs a way to better measure their value and communicate it.

The Model Reviewed

The EDGE has adopted the process presented in Chapter 13 as a way of better measuring and reporting its impact. As will be described, it follows the model to develop a better understanding of the context in which its work is situated, to describe its work in terms of a Situated Logic Model, to develop and implement an outcome measuring system, and to reflect on the process to inform future work at its organization (see Figure 14.1).

Context Mapping

Context analysis requires that the EDGE understands the policy issues defining the context within which it operates and the stakeholders associated with those policy issues. The context mapping steps provide a way for the EDGE to identify and define aspects of the policy issues that its work affects, and the stakeholders it intersects with, in order to provide a holistic base for evaluating the impact of its organization.

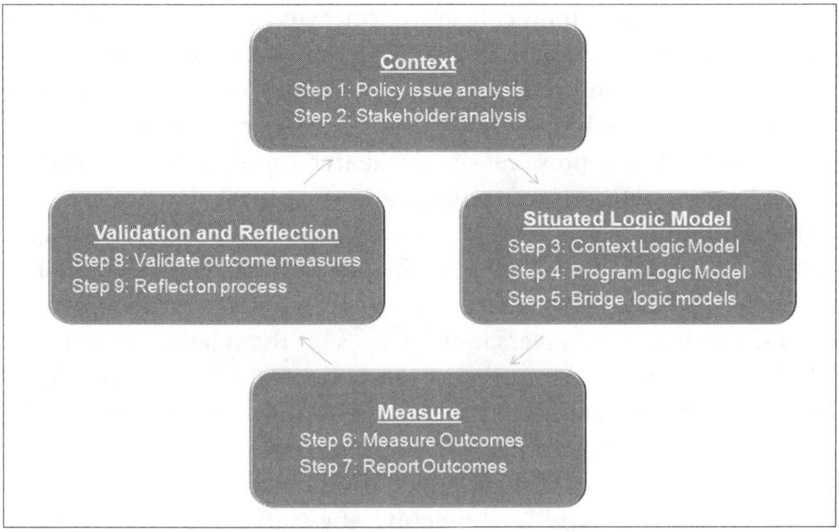

Figure 14.1 Community Technology Impact Measurement Process Model

Step 1: Policy Issue Analysis

The EDGE staff are active members of the community. The EDGE staff regularly collaborate with and attend the meetings of other community groups and city, county, and state agencies. The staff participates in conferences, subscribes to industry related email lists, and attends community events. Additionally, staff members actively engage in monitoring the local newspapers and industry-related journals. The culture of the EDGE is to share news among co-workers, and discussion of the news comes up frequently during team meetings. The EDGE staff also make contact with city- and state-elected officials to keep them apprised of their work and to open up dialogue regarding important policy issues affecting their community.

These activities create an environment in which the EDGE staff members stay current on relevant happenings in their community and, more importantly, on the public policy issues relevant to their work and the community. The staff are not only knowledgeable regarding those issues but understand the relevance to their work and make it a priority to discuss this relevance in staff meetings.

To start the process, the EDGE schedules three 2-hour meetings to conduct the policy issue analysis. During the first meeting, members identify the following major issues confronting their community: the economy, unemployment, education and the dropout rate, homelessness, poverty, and crime. The staff then collect information regarding these issues and the ways that the work of the EDGE impacts these issues.

During the second meeting, the EDGE staff present the information collected, which was drawn from a variety of sources including newspaper articles, press releases, research reports, journal articles, annual reports of nonprofit organizations, statistical analysis of the community, interviews with stakeholders and other organizations, as well as anecdotal information. Staff consider the research gathered on each of the issues and discuss the EDGE's role in addressing these issues. Much of the conversation focuses on the relative importance of the issues to the community and the EDGE's unique role in addressing those issues. After the information has been discussed by the group, the staff members are asked to reflect on the meeting and think about the issues that should be prioritized.

During the third and final meeting, the staff engage in a spirited discussion of how these problems should be assigned in the priority list. Some members of the staff believe that all issues should be covered in the policy analysis, and others vote for focused effort on a select few areas of interest. This discussion results in the EDGE staff agreeing that resources should focus on a select few areas of interest in their first effort to use the process model, and staff agree to focus on unemployment and the economy. They feel that this is the most pressing need facing the community and an area where they are making a significant impact.

Step 2: Stakeholder Analysis

Next, the EDGE staff collect information on the stakeholders associated with the issues of unemployment and economic development. Staff members recognize that stakeholders play an important role in determining what gets done, by whom, and how, and that their work is integrally tied to the work of these stakeholders.

A meeting is called to discuss the stakeholder issue, and staff members use a whiteboard to create a diagram listing all the stakeholders that intersect with their organization and the relationships between these organizations. Some of the stakeholders identified are:

- State government
- City government
- Federal government

- Numerous nonprofit agencies
- Foundations
- Healthcare industry
- Manufacturing industry
- Technology industry
- Education sector
- Citizens
- Employees
- The unemployed
- Participants in the EDGE's programs

The staff members discuss each of the stakeholders in terms of their relationship to the chosen policy issue and ways in which the work of the EDGE addresses these issues.

Some of the stakeholders that the EDGE identifies are experiencing changes due to the dynamics of the local economy. For example, one of the companies in the Edgeville manufacturing industry, an industry that is dominated by five large companies, has recently declared bankruptcy, and two others have announced plans for large layoffs. The impact on the community's workforce and unemployment rates will be significant. On the other hand, the healthcare and technology sectors are relatively strong with prospects for growth.

As a result of these changes, a coalition of nonprofits, foundations, and government agencies forms an initiative called "Edgeville Works." This initiative focuses on assessing and enhancing the skills needed by workers in the growing industries and providing job retraining support for the unemployed. The initiative's development effort is sponsored by a major foundation that partners with the city, several job training nonprofit organizations, and leading employers in the healthcare and technology sectors. The EDGE staff determine that by situating their work in terms of this initiative they could make a strong case for the impact of their work on some of the most important issues facing the community.

The Situated Logic Model

Following the completion of the first set of steps, the EDGE staff have developed a thorough understanding of an important policy issue confronting the community. They are now faced with the task of visually mapping out the work of Edgeville Works (context logic model) and the work of the EDGE CTC (program logic model) within the context of the identified policy issue of unemployment and the economy. They will then need to map out the relationships between the context logic model and the program logic model to create the Situated Logic Model. The EDGE staff schedule a meeting to work on the processes necessary for carrying out each step of the Situated Logic Model.

Step 3: Context Logic Model

The next step in creating the Situated Logic Model involves developing a logic model that represents the EDGE's understanding of the logic of its chosen context, the Edgeville Works Initiative. The stated mission of the initiative is "to strengthen the local economy and reduce unemployment by identifying employment opportunities, assessing skills demand, promoting job training, and facilitating coordination among stakeholders." The EDGE team begins by mapping out the participants, resources, and actions that make up the Edgeville Works Initiative.

Staff members then set about creating a logic model, depicted in Figure 14.2, that describes the work done by the initiative. The inputs include public and private dollars, human resources, and the credibility and clout of the city and foundation sponsoring the effort. The activities engaged in include developing a database that lists both the job opportunities in the healthcare and technology industries and the skills required for these positions. It also presents the work done to coordinate the gathering of job opportunity information, the process of working with workforce training systems to provide skills required in the healthcare and technology industries, and public outreach efforts aimed at unemployed workers. Outputs of the initiative's work are a searchable database of job listings, inventory of skills needed in the industries, and marketing of the job database and opportunities in the healthcare field. Outcomes include an increased number of people being trained to gain skills in the healthcare field, placement of workers in healthcare jobs, and a more coordinated

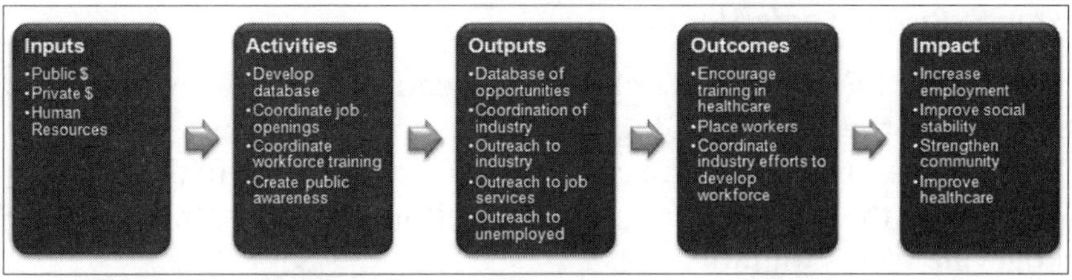

Figure 14.2 Edgeville Works Initiative Logic Model

industry that is actively developing means of training a better workforce. Finally, the impact of these efforts on the community is increased employment, a more stable social structure correlated with higher employment, and improved healthcare as a result of more and better trained healthcare workers.

Step 4: Program Logic Model

The EDGE staff now turn to defining the work of the EDGE itself in terms of a logic model. The logic model for the EDGE CTC, illustrated in Figure 14.3, represents the processes the organization engages in toward impacting its clientele. The inputs include funding from a variety of sources, staff working hours, and the equipping of a computer lab. The organization engages in activities such as providing access to computers and delivering training. As a result of the training and access to technology, the output of its work is measured by number of hours trained, skills taught, resumes written, and job applications submitted. Finally, the outcomes of its effort result in clients placed in jobs as well as skills learned and used. The impact of this work on the clients is their ability to better provide for themselves and their families, as well as the positive social benefits of being employed, including increased confidence, which impacts other areas of their lives.

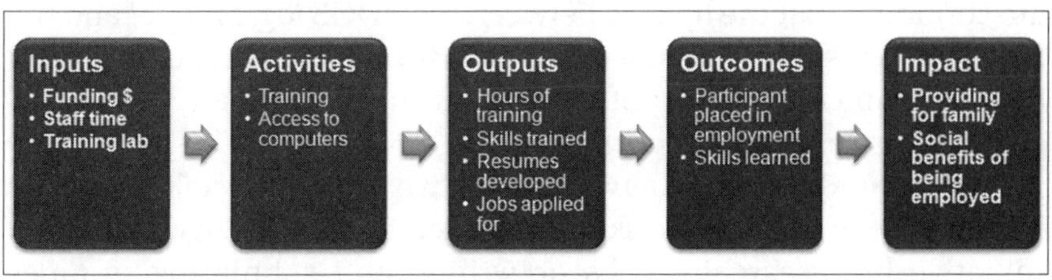

Figure 14.3 Program Logic Model

Step 5: Bridge Logic Models

Finally, the EDGE defines linkages between the Edgeville Works logic model and the EDGE CTC logic model, as shown in Figure 14.4. These linkages clearly support the contentions that the work of the EDGE is critical to the work of larger policy efforts such as those of the Edgeville Works Initiative.

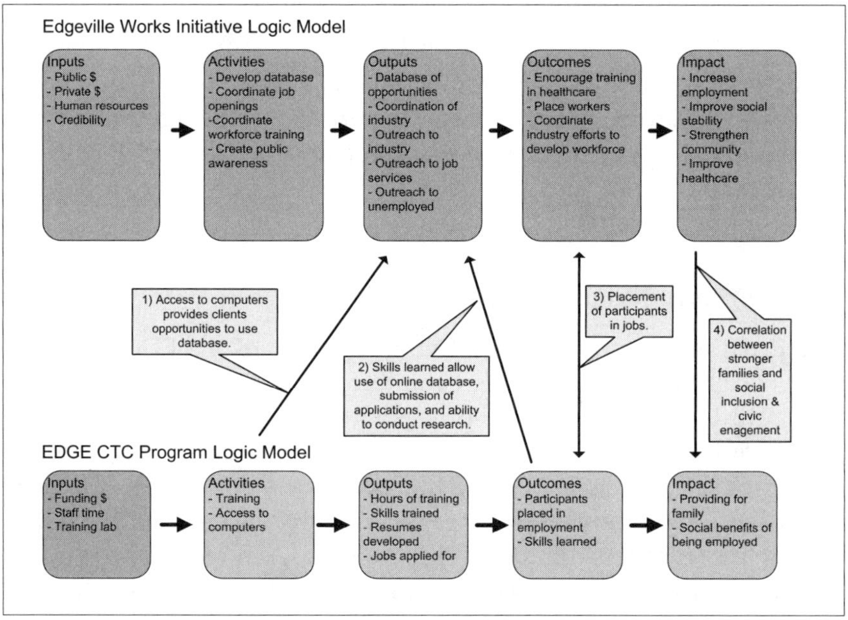

Figure 14.4 Bridging the Logic Models

The first linkage shown between the two models is access to computers, allowing job seekers to use the database built by the Edgeville Works Initiative. Providing access to computers and on-site staff to instruct clients in their use are critical factors in reaching the populations targeted by the Edgeville Works Initiative. EDGE staff members are confident that the linkage between the EDGE logic model and the Edgeville Works logic model is logically sound and can be measured by identifying the number of participants in the program that access the database and are supported.

The second linkage between the two models establishes the importance of gaining the skills to participate in the Edgeville Works Initiative by researching jobs or writing and submitting resumes through the application process. This linkage could also be measured by tracking the number of participants in the program who apply for jobs through the Edgeville Works Initiative.

The third linkage focuses directly on the outcomes of both programs, which share the objective of placing program participants in jobs. By working together, both programs could recognize and actively address the outcome measure of job placement. This linkage is important as a shared goal and also one that can be measured and reported.

The final linkage identified by the EDGE staff focuses on the impact of the work of both programs. The modeled impact measures for the Edgeville Works Initiative focus on benefits to the community. The Edgeville Works Initiative target objectives are improving the community as a whole, which includes the economy, the healthcare industry, and the overall health of the community. The EDGE CTC program logic model quantifies impacts associated with the individuals it serves. It recognizes that the impact to individuals has long-term benefits and affects their immediate surroundings. Its Situated Logic Model shows how these two ways of understanding impact are highly correlated. The impact measures can be measured but need to also be grounded in the literature that supports the logic implicit to the model.

Outcome Measurement

The EDGE staff are now ready to identify the outcome measures and report those measures to the public. They hold a meeting to discuss the process of measuring outcomes associated with the linkages between the two models and also to figure out how they can report those outcomes to the larger community.

Step 6: Measure Outcomes

The program logic model identifies skill acquisition and job placement as outcomes derived from the EDGE's efforts. Systems were put into place to measure these outcomes and report them. Using the Situated Logic Model approach, the EDGE sets up systems to measure and report outcomes associated with the linkages identified in the Situated Logic Model. The following types of measures are determined by the EDGE staff to be necessary:

1. The first link could be measured by the number of times participants used the computer lab to access the workforce database. Data for this measure could be collected using usage tracking tools, surveys of use, or informal observation. This data could be compiled to demonstrate the use of computers to access the workforce database.
2. The EDGE staff determine the need to identify the skills required to access the database, apply for jobs online, and do research. They determine that they would need to measure the times that participants used these skills. Measuring the skills would require a skills assessment to identify which skills are required to use the online workforce database. Once these skills are determined, a skills assessment could be conducted to determine which participants have gained the skills and used them to interact with the database.
3. The placement of participants in jobs is an outcome measure of both logic models. Identifying the number of EDGE CTC participants who gain employment through the Edgeville Works Initiative is an important statistic that demonstrates the success of the CTC program in conjunction with the efforts of the Edgeville Works Initiative. It also demonstrates the alignment of shared objectives between the two programs.
4. Lastly, EDGE staff determine that impact measures reflect the impact of the programs individually and working together. The impact measures are less concrete than the other measures; however, surveys or interviews could be used to elicit information regarding individual well-being and how that well-being translates into the positive community indicators such as social engagement.

Step 7: Report Outcomes

The EDGE now sets about reporting the outcome measures to policymakers and funders using the Situated Logic Model. Staff members feel that this would be the best way of illustrating the linkages between their program and the broader work of Edgeville Works. In their presentation, staff first explain that the EDGE CTC is a program that works within the community and collaboratively with numerous other efforts. They highlight their collaborative efforts with the Edgeville Works Initiative as one of their particularly important efforts, one that enables workers to participate and benefit from the Edgeville Works Initiative. They point out that these two programs share common objectives and work together toward achieving those objectives, resulting in a significant impact to individuals, families, and their communities.

To be more specific, the EDGE identifies 70 participants who used the computers to access the workforce development database. In order to access and use the database, participants needed to have basic internet skills including using a web browser, developing queries to search a database, storing search results, using a word processor to create a resume, and using the internet to fill out the online applications and submit the resume. The EDGE recorded 62 participants who used these skills to apply online for the advertised jobs. Of the 62 participants, 25 were placed in jobs. These 25 people were given a survey after 6 months of employment and found to have much higher scores of happiness, well being, and confidence. They were also found to be more socially connected in the community. In their report, EDGE staff members point to research that supports the view that employment leads to happiness, increased confidence, and greater engagement in the community.

Validation and Reflective Practices

The EDGE staff dedicate two additional meetings to the final two steps of validation and reflection.

Step 8: Validate Outcome Measures

The EDGE staff consider the outcome measures developed to determine whether these outcome measures are:

1. Accurately measuring what they are intended to measure
2. The best measures of the outcome link

For example, the EDGE staff consider the assessment instrument or approach used to determine participant's acquisition of skills. Staff members consider whether skills are being accurately measured and ask questions about whether the current approach is overestimating or underestimating skill acquisition. The staff also consider whether there are different approaches that might be used to determine skills acquired.

Secondly, the EDGE staff consider whether the skills measured are the best measures to represent the linkage between the EDGE program and Edgeville Works Initiative. These inquiries center on questions such as:

- What skills are needed to use the online workforce development resources?
- Are there other skills that should be considered?
- If so, how might these skills be measured?
- Are there skills being measured that are not appropriate?

Step 9: Reflect on Process

Lastly, the EDGE staff reflect on the entire process. Staff consider questions regarding the success of each step. For example, staff members ask the following questions about the first seven steps:

- Step 1, Policy Issues: Is our original understanding of the policy issues affecting our community accurate? Have other policy issues emerged? Should we expand our understanding to include other efforts addressing policy issues in our community?
- Step 2, Stakeholders: Did we identify the primary stakeholders? Have additional stakeholders emerged? Are there stakeholders who were considered who are not as relevant? How accurate is our understanding of stakeholders? Have we learned new information about stakeholders that we should consider in the use of our model?
- Step 3, Context Logic Model: Did we capture the context of our CTC accurately? Are there additional aspects that should be captured? Are there aspects that we no longer consider relevant?
- Step 4, Program Logic Model: Did we capture our work accurately? Did we identify the important and relevant aspects of our work? Is the logic model representative of our work? Are we missing anything that should be captured?

- Step 5, Bridging Models: Do the linkages we used to situate our work within the context of identified policy issues make sense? Are there other linkages that should be identified and represented? Are there linkages that should be removed and are not as important and relevant as others?
- Step 6, Outcome Measures: How did the process of collecting outcome measure data go? Are there ways we can improve this process? What is the cost of collecting the data? How well was the data collected?
- Step 7, Reporting: How effective are our reporting mechanisms? How difficult is it for us to report data? How might our reporting mechanisms be improved? Are the right people getting the information needed? Is the information being communicated effectively?

The EDGE staff reflect on the process as a whole and its impact on their organization and their efforts in the community. The information collected helps staff brainstorm ways to improve and develop their organization:

1. How effective have we been as an organization supporting work done toward achieving the larger policy issues facing our community?
2. How effective have we been in communicating the value of the work we have done? How might we communicate that information better?
3. How responsive has the community been to our message? What have been some of our successes in communicating our message? What have been some of our failings?
4. What are the most important ways we can improve on the modeling approach used? What are some of the shortcomings? What are some of the strengths?

Conclusion

By engaging in the Community Technology Impact Measurement Process Model, the EDGE staff were able to better understand their impact on the community as understood by their role in addressing communitywide policy efforts. The exercise allowed them to make a strong case for the importance and relevance of their work in making other community efforts possible. They were able to articulate and report these findings to funders and policymakers in the community. As a result of this exercise, the value they were creating is made more explicit.

CHAPTER 15

Resources and Further Exploration

Michael Crandall and Karen E. Fisher

This book has covered a great deal of territory, from the brief description of the community organizing efforts by Washington State's community technology providers and the successful enactment of legislation providing a definition of their work and funding to support future activities to a description of the findings from our research and field work to a theoretical framework that can be used by others to carry this work forward in their own communities.

In closing, we provide a number of resources that may be of use to those who are working in the area of digital inclusion, and want to become part of the larger efforts going on in their state or the nation. We hope that many of you will be inspired by the findings presented in this book to join in the work that so many people are doing to bring needed services to the communities they inhabit and help to make digital inclusion a reality for all segments of our population. Further work on this research can be seen on our project website at cis.washington.edu/usimpact/projects/ccn-study. In the words of the sites themselves, here are brief descriptions of some useful resources.

Advocacy Organizations

- Alliance for Community Technology (www.communitytechnology.org) – The Alliance for Community Technology was launched in 1997 as a strategic partnership between the W. K. Kellogg Foundation and the University of Michigan through its new School of Information.

- The California Community Technology Policy Group (CCTPG; www.cctpg.org) – CCTPG is a statewide network of diverse community-based organizations advocating for new public policies to improve underserved communities' access to advanced technologies.
- Communities Connect Network (CCN; www.communities connect.org) – CCN was created as a public-private collaborative for the purpose of discovering and implementing sustainability mechanisms for Washington State's community technology field.
- Community Technology Alliance (www.ctagroup.org) – Community Technology Alliance, formerly Santa Clara Valley Multi Service Center, was established in 1991 as a direct result of recommendations made by the Santa Clara County Homeless Task Force Study in 1989, which recommended the development of a system of communication and collaboration among shelter providers. Community Technology Alliance is a partnership among shelter and emergency service providers, specialized nonprofits, Santa Clara County, and the City of San Jose.
- Community Technology Centers' Network (CTCNet; www.ctcnet.org) – The CTCNet is a national membership network of community technology centers (CTCs) and other nonprofits, united in their commitment to provide technology access and education to underserved communities. CTCNet works through the CTC Network to provide resources and advocacy to improve the quality and sustainability of CTCs.
- Community Technology Network (CTN; www.ctnbay area.org) – CTN was formed on August 14, 2001, at a regional community technology meeting convened by CompuMentor under the auspices of the America Connects Consortium. A regional collaborative, CTN helps community technology practitioners leverage and improve their work products through peer feedback and support. In this shared space, practitioners develop work products, explore ideas, and directly disseminate resources to support community technology practices and services.

- Connect Ohio (www.connectohio.org) – Connect Ohio is a public-private partnership that partners with technology-minded businesses, government entities, and universities to accelerate technology in the state and close the digital divide.
- Illinois Community Technology Coalition (ilCTC; ilctc.org) – The ilCTC is a network of volunteers and professionals in the community technology sector. It emerged through the work of the Illinois Community Technology Consortium funded by the Illinois Community Technology Fund over a 3-year period.
- Microsoft Unlimited Potential (www.microsoft.com/unlimitedpotential) – Microsoft Unlimited Potential combines advanced technologies and strong partnerships with governments, international organizations, nongovernmental organizations, educational institutions, and technology and service partners. Ultimately their mission is to enable sustained social and economic opportunity for those at the middle and bottom of the world's economic pyramid—the next 5 billion people.
- Seattle's Community Technology Program (www.seattle.gov/tech) – The City of Seattle is committed to promoting a technology healthy community. This includes ensuring that residents have the information technology training and access needed to ensure civic and cultural participation, employment, and lifelong learning.
- ZeroDivide (www.zerodivide.org) – ZeroDivide was founded in 1998 as a result of the groundbreaking advocacy work and coalition building of 134 community organizations during the merger of two telecommunications companies, Pacific Bell and SBC Communications.

Research Centers

- Center for Community Technology Services (CCTS; ccts.ubalt.edu) – In 2003, with the backing of the University of Baltimore, CCTS started to help Baltimore area nonprofits increase their ability to use technology, strengthen their organizations, and improve their service delivery.

- Center for Information and Society (CIS; www.cis.washington.edu) – The University of Washington's CIS studies the design, use, and impact of information and communication technologies on individuals and communities around the world. Their research focuses on disadvantaged and underrepresented populations, and on four main areas of inquiry: access, development, culture, and policy.
- Community Informatics Initiative (CII; www.cii.uiuc.edu) – The CII works with people to develop information and communication technologies to achieve their goals. It fosters collaborations across campus, local, national and international communities. The CII builds innovative community networks, community technology centers, software, and library services.
- Community Informatics Research Network (www.ciresearch.net) – The purpose of the network is to promote and represent community informatics and community networking research internationally. Community Informatics lies at two crossroads: bringing together people concerned with electronically enabling communities: local, virtual, and communities of practice; and structuring collaborations between researchers and practitioners, including industry, in these three domains and to support a community-based approach to the implementation of ICT systems and services including Internet access and responses to the Digital Divide.
- Community Tech Wikispace (communitytech.wikispaces.com) – This site was originally developed to support the Community Informatics wildcard session at the 3rd Annual iSchools Conference (February 28–March 1, UCLA, 2008). It is now serving as the space for those interested in participating in future community informatics activities associated with the iSchools Conferences and the iSchools community.
- Information Policy Research Program (IPRP; www3.fis.utoronto.ca/research/iprp) – IPRP is an ongoing program

of research examining key public policy issues, notably access, privacy, and governance.

- Prairienet (www.prairienet.org) – Prairienet, founded in 1993, is a member- and donation-supported community information network for Champaign-Urbana by the Graduate School of Library and Information Science at the University of Illinois at Urbana-Champaign.
- Rob Kling Center for Social Informatics (rkcsi.indiana.edu) – Social Informatics refers to the body of research and study that examines social aspects of computerization, including the roles of information technology in social and organizational change, the uses of information technologies in social contexts, and the ways that the social organization of information technologies is influenced by social forces and social practices.
- University of California-Berkeley Center for Information and Communication Technologies and Development (www.ischool.berkeley.edu/programs/centers/ictd) – Research on Information and Communication Technologies and Development (ICTD) at the School of Information follows several distinct trajectories: First, to *understand* current processes of technology diffusion and adoption in developing regions. Second, to *act* through the design and deployment of information systems in close collaboration with the communities they are meant to support. Finally, to *reshape* the dialogue about the role of technology in the global economic and political processes that affect developing regions.
- University of Michigan Information Use in Communities Research Theme (www.si.umich.edu/research/area.htm?AreaID=5) – This area involves understanding and supporting, particularly with contextual approaches, how information flows, information resources, and information technologies form, maintain, and serve geographic and cyber-communities and communities of practice.

Washington State Law 6438

CERTIFICATION OF ENROLLMENT

ENGROSSED SECOND SUBSTITUTE SENATE BILL 6438

Chapter 262, Laws of 2008

60th Legislature
2008 Regular Session

TECHNOLOGY OPPORTUNITIES--HIGH-SPEED INTERNET

EFFECTIVE DATE: 06/12/08

Passed by the Senate March 12, 2008
YEAS 45 NAYS 0

BRAD OWEN

President of the Senate

Passed by the House March 11, 2008
YEAS 95 NAYS 0

FRANK CHOPP

Speaker of the House of Representatives

Approved March 31, 2008, 11:25 a.m.

CHRISTINE GREGOIRE

Governor of the State of Washington

CERTIFICATE

I, Thomas Hoemann, Secretary of the Senate of the State of Washington, do hereby certify that the attached is **ENGROSSED SECOND SUBSTITUTE SENATE BILL 6438** as passed by the Senate and the House of Representatives on the dates hereon set forth.

THOMAS HOEMANN

Secretary

FILED

April 1, 2008

Secretary of State
State of Washington

ENGROSSED SECOND SUBSTITUTE SENATE BILL 6438

AS AMENDED BY THE HOUSE

Passed Legislature - 2008 Regular Session

State of Washington **60th Legislature** **2008 Regular Session**

By Senate Ways & Means (originally sponsored by Senators Kohl-Welles, Rockefeller, Oemig, Honeyford, Murray, Delvin, and Pridemore)

READ FIRST TIME 02/12/08.

AN ACT Relating to a statewide high-speed internet deployment and adoption initiative; adding new sections to chapter 43.105 RCW; adding a new chapter to Title 28B RCW; and creating new sections.

BE IT ENACTED BY THE LEGISLATURE OF THE STATE OF WASHINGTON:

NEW SECTION. **Sec. 1.** (1) The legislature finds and declares the following:

(a) The deployment and adoption of high-speed internet services and information technology has resulted in enhanced economic development and public safety for the state's communities, improved health care and educational opportunities, and a better quality of life for the state's residents;

(b) Continued progress in the deployment and adoption of high-speed internet services and other advanced telecommunications services, both land-based and wireless, is vital to ensuring Washington remains competitive and continues to create business and job growth; and

(c) That the state must encourage and support strategic partnerships of public, private, nonprofit, and community-based sectors in the continued growth and development of high-speed internet services and information technology for state residents and businesses.

(2) Therefore, in order to begin advancing the state towards further growth and development of high-speed internet in the state, and to ensure a better quality of life for all state residents, it is the legislature's intent to conduct a statewide needs assessment of broadband internet resources through an open dialogue with all interested parties, including providers, unions, businesses, community organizations, local governments, and state agencies. The legislature intends to use this needs assessment in guiding future plans on how to ensure that every resident in Washington state may gain access to high-speed internet services and, as part of this effort, to address digital literacy and technology training needs of low-income and technology underserved residents of the state through state support of community technology programs.

NEW SECTION. **Sec. 2.** (1) After the broadband study authorized by the legislature in 2007 has been completed, or by July 15, 2008, the department of information services, in coordination with the department of community, trade, and economic development and the utilities and transportation commission, shall convene a work group to develop a high-speed internet deployment and adoption strategy for the state.

(2) The department of information services shall invite representatives from the following organizations to participate in the work group:

(a) Representatives of public, private, and nonprofit agencies and organizations representing economic development, local community development, local government, community planning, technology planning, education, and health care;

(b) Representatives of telecommunications providers, technology companies, telecommunications unions, public utilities, and relevant private sector entities;

(c) Representatives of community-based organizations; and

(d) Representatives of other relevant entities as the department of information services may deem appropriate.

(3) The department of information services shall, in consultation with the work group, develop a high-speed internet deployment and adoption strategy to accomplish the following objectives:

(a) Create and regularly update a detailed, geographic information system map at the census block level of the high-speed internet services and other relevant telecommunications and information technology services owned or leased by public entities in the state with instructions on how proprietary and competitively sensitive data will be handled, stored, and used. Development of this geographic information system map may include collaboration with students and faculty at community colleges and universities in the state. The statewide inventory must, at a minimum, detail:

(i) The physical location of all high-speed internet infrastructure owned or leased by public entities;

(ii) The amount of excess capacity available; and

(iii) Whether the high-speed internet infrastructure is active or inactive;

(b) Work collaboratively with telecommunications providers and internet service providers to assess, create, and regularly update a geographic information system map at the census block level of the privately owned high-speed internet infrastructure in the state, with instructions on how proprietary and competitively sensitive data will be handled, stored, and used;

(c) Combine the geographic information system map of high-speed internet infrastructure owned by public entities with the geographic information system map of high-speed internet infrastructure owned by private entities to create and regularly update a statewide inventory of all high-speed internet infrastructure in the state;

(d) Use the geographic information system map of all high-speed internet infrastructure in the state, both public and privately owned or leased, to identify and regularly update the geographic gaps in high-speed internet service, including an assessment of the population located in each of the geographic gaps;

(e) Spur the development of high-speed internet resources in the state, which may include, but is not limited to, soliciting funding in the form of grants or donations; establishing technology literacy programs in conjunction with institutions of higher education; establishing low-cost hardware and software purchasing programs; and developing loan programs targeting small businesses or businesses located in underserved areas;

(f) Track statewide residential and business adoption of high-speed internet, computers, and related information technology, including an identification of barriers to adoption;

(g) Build and facilitate local technology planning teams and partnerships with members representing cross-sections of the community, which may include participation from the following organizations: Representatives of business, telecommunications unions, K-12 education, community colleges, local economic development organizations, health care, libraries, universities, community-based organizations, local governments, tourism, parks and recreation, and agriculture;

(h) Use the local technology planning teams and partnerships to:

(i) Conduct a needs assessment; and

(ii) Work collaboratively with high-speed internet providers and technology companies across the state to encourage deployment and use, especially in unserved areas, through use of local demand aggregation, mapping analysis, and creation of market intelligence to improve the investment rationale and business case; and

(i) Work with Washington State University extension pursuant to section 6 of this act to establish low-cost programs to improve computer ownership, technology literacy, and high-speed internet access for disenfranchised or unserved populations across the state.

(4) By September 1, 2008, the department of information services shall provide a status update to the telecommunications committees in the house of representatives and the senate, outlining the progress made to date by the work group and the issues remaining to be considered.

(5) By December 1, 2008, the department of information services shall complete the high-speed internet deployment and adoption strategy and provide a report to the fiscal and telecommunications committees in the house of representatives and the senate, the governor, and the office of financial management. The main objective of the report is to outline, based on the efforts of the work group, what legislation is needed in order to implement the high-speed internet deployment and adoption strategy, including a range of potential funding requests to accompany the legislation. Specifically, the report shall include the following:

(a) Benchmarks, performance measures, milestones, deliverables, timelines, and such other indicators of performance and progress as are necessary to guide development and implementation of the high-speed internet deployment and adoption strategy, both short term and long term, including an assessment of the amount of funding needed to accomplish a baseline assessment of the high-speed internet infrastructure owned by public and private entities of the state in an eighteen-month period; and

(b) Ways to structure and appropriately scale and phase development and implementation of the high-speed internet deployment and adoption strategy so as to link to, leverage, and otherwise synchronize with other relevant and related funding, technology, capital initiatives, investments, and opportunities.

NEW SECTION. **Sec. 3.** A new section is added to chapter 43.105 RCW to read as follows:

(1) For purposes of compliance with section 2 of this act or any subsequent high-speed internet deployment and adoption initiative, the department of information services, the department of community, trade, and economic development, the utilities and transportation commission, and any other government agent or agency shall not gather or request any information related to high-speed internet infrastructure or service from providers of telecommunications or high-speed internet services that is classified by the provider as proprietary or competitively sensitive.

(2) Nothing in this section may be construed as limiting the authority of a state agency or local government to gather or request information from providers of telecommunications or high-speed internet services for other purposes pursuant to its statutory authority.

NEW SECTION. **Sec. 4.** Nothing in this act may be construed as giving the department of information services or any other entities any additional authority, regulatory or otherwise, over providers of telecommunications and information technology.

NEW SECTION. **Sec. 5.** A new section is added to chapter 43.105 RCW to read as follows:

(1) By January 1, 2009, the department, in consultation with Washington State University, shall identify and make publicly available a web directory of public facilities that provide community technology programs throughout the state.

(2) For the purposes of this section, "community technology program" has the same meaning as in section 7 of this act.

<u>NEW SECTION.</u> **Sec. 6.** The community technology opportunity program is created to support the efforts of community technology programs throughout the state. The community technology opportunity program must be administered by the Washington State University extension, in consultation with the department of information services. The Washington State University extension may contract for services in order to carry out the extension's obligations under this section.

(1) In implementing the community technology opportunity program the administrator must, to the extent funds are appropriated for this purpose:

(a) Provide organizational and capacity building support to community technology programs throughout the state, and identify and facilitate the availability of other public and private sources of funds to enhance the purposes of the program and the work of community technology programs. No more than fifteen percent of funds received by the administrator for the program may be expended on these functions;

(b) Establish a competitive grant program and provide grants to community technology programs to provide training and skill-building opportunities; access to hardware and software; internet connectivity; assistance in the adoption of information and communication technologies in low-income and underserved areas of the state; and development of locally relevant content and delivery of vital services through technology.

(2) Grant applicants must:

(a) Provide evidence that the applicant is a nonprofit entity or a public entity that is working in partnership with a nonprofit entity;

(b) Define the geographic area or population to be served;

(c) Include in the application the results of a needs assessment addressing, in the geographic area or among the population to be served: The impact of inadequacies in technology access or knowledge, barriers faced, and services needed;

(d) Explain in detail the strategy for addressing the needs identified and an implementation plan including objectives, tasks, and benchmarks for the applicant and the role that other organizations will play in assisting the applicant's efforts;

(e) Provide evidence of matching funds and resources, which are equivalent to at least one-quarter of the grant amount committed to the applicant's strategy;

(f) Provide evidence that funds applied for, if received, will be used to provide effective delivery of community technology services in alignment with the goals of this program and to increase the applicant's level of effort beyond the current level; and

(g) Comply with such other requirements as the administrator establishes.

(3) The administrator may use no more than ten percent of funds received for the community technology opportunity program to cover administrative expenses.

(4) The administrator must establish expected program outcomes for each grant recipient and must require grant recipients to provide an annual accounting of program outcomes.

NEW SECTION. **Sec. 7.** The definitions in this section apply throughout this chapter unless the context clearly requires otherwise.

(1) "Administrator" means the community technology opportunity program administrator designated by the Washington State University extension.

(2) "Community technology program" means a program, including a digital inclusion program, engaged in diffusing information and communications technology in local communities, particularly in underserved areas. These programs may include, but are not limited to, programs that provide education and skill-building opportunities, hardware and software, internet connectivity, and development of locally relevant content and delivery of vital services through technology.

NEW SECTION. **Sec. 8.** The Washington community technology opportunity account is established in the state treasury. Donated funds from private and public sources may be deposited into the account. Expenditures from the account may be used only for the operation of the community technology opportunity program as provided in section 6 of this act. Only the administrator or the administrator's designee may authorize expenditures from the account.

NEW SECTION. **Sec. 9.** Sections 6 through 8 of this act constitute a new chapter in Title 28B RCW.

NEW SECTION. **Sec. 10.** If sections 1 through 5 of this act become null and void, the department of information services shall include high-speed internet adoption and deployment in its 2009-2011 strategic plan.

NEW SECTION. **Sec. 11.** If specific funding for the purposes of sections 1 through 5 of this act, referencing sections 1 through 5 of this act by bill or chapter number, is not provided by June 30, 2008, in the omnibus appropriations act, sections 1 through 5 of this act are null and void.

Passed by the Senate March 12, 2008.
Passed by the House March 11, 2008.
Approved by the Governor March 31, 2008.
Filed in Office of Secretary of State April 1, 2008.

Presentation to Senate Economic Development, Trade and Management Committee

communities • connect • network
advancing community technology in washington state

Digital Inclusion in Action:

How Washington's community technology nonprofits provide access, literacy and content

Senate Economic Development, Trade & Management Committee
November 30, 2007

communities • connect • network
advancing community technology in washington state

Communities Connect Network

- What is Communities Connect Network?
  - A statewide coalition of public and private organizations working to ensure that Washington state is a leader in "digital inclusion" – the movement to ensure that all individuals have access and the skills to use the Internet and information technologies.
  - Lead partners include the City of Seattle Department of Information Technology, the University of Washington Information School, OneEconomy Corporation, Washington State University Extension Center to Bridge the Digital Divide, Stone Soup, and NPower Seattle
- What does CCN do?
  - Supports service providers
  - Conducts research
  - Disseminates and trains community technology providers on best practices
  - Brings awareness of the need for and impact of digital inclusion to public officials, business leaders, and the citizens of Washington state
  - Learn more at http://communitiesconnect.org

November 30, 2007 2

communities • connect • network
advancing community technology in washington state

Removing Barriers to Digital Inclusion

- CCN and its members have adopted this framework to help individuals, small businesses and non-profits join the information age
  - *Providing **access** to computers and the internet*
    - Availability, cost, ease of use for connectivity to the Internet, and end-user hardware and software
  - *Building **literacy** in using computer and internet technologies*
    - Skills required in order to utilize the equipment and Internet effectively for essential services, education, employment, civic engagement and cultural participation
  - *Making meaningful and useful **content and services** available*
    - Services available for those in need, culturally and educationally appropriate design, marketing and placement appropriate to reach underserved communities, and enabling of content production and distribution by lower capacity residents, businesses and organizations

November 30, 2007 3

communities • connect • network
advancing community technology in washington state

A Study of CT in Washington State

- Last summer, UW conducted a phone survey across 211 agencies in the state identified as community technology providers. 47of these agencies completed the survey, and 7 sites were visited for more in-depth study.
- This was combined with earlier data to provide a snapshot of CT in Washington State
- Findings indicate both the impact that CT is having on communities, as well as barriers being faced

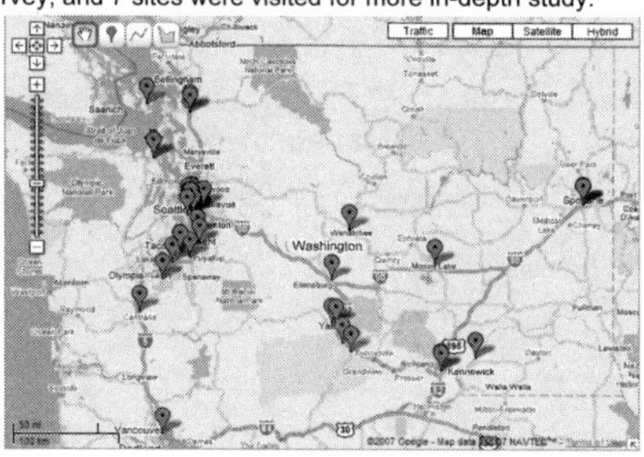

November 30, 2007 4

communities • connect • network
advancing community technology in washington state

Findings: How Many People Served?

- Based on information from ***about half*** of the known community technology providers in the state– we know that these agencies serve:

99,467 unique users per year

Weekly counts show that ***on average, a user visits 14 times*** during the year

Resulting in an estimated total of
1,392,538 visits per year

November 30, 2007 5

communities • connect • network
advancing community technology in washington state

User Demographics

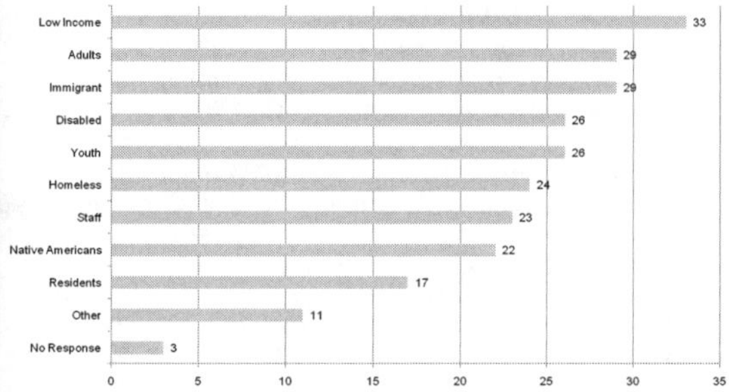

Responses from 47 surveyed programs (multiple audiences per site)

November 30, 2007 6

communities • connect • network
advancing community technology in washington state

About the Users

- **How long have users been coming?**
  - Approximately one third had been coming to the center for one year or less, just over 36% attended for 2 years, and 27% had used the center for 3 or more years.
- **How much time do they spend there?**
  - The majority of users (62%) stated that the average amount of time spent at the center ranged from less than an hour per week up to 6 hours per week, while 24% indicated that they used the center 7 or more hours per week.
- **Are users satisfied with services?**
  - 88% percent of users indicated that they will continue to use the CTCs. Furthermore, the value users find in the centers was reflected in their recommendations to others. Almost 69% of CTC recommendations were directed toward friends or acquaintances, 19% went to family and 13% percent referred to others

November 30, 2007 7

communities • connect • network
advancing community technology in washington state

Individual Benefits

- **Employment/Economic Benefits**
  - Developed job skills that prepared them for getting a job
  - Empowered to obtain additional technical skills
  - Helped gain employment

- *"The center offers a business training course that covers such issues as developing a business plan, planning finances, and determining whether a business idea is feasible. Classes include an introduction to Computers, and various Business Classes that integrate computer skills. For example, users can learn Word and develop a business plan, learn Excel to complete cash flow projections, or learn Web design and make a website for their business."* Washington CASH, Seattle

November 30, 2007 8

communities • connect • network
advancing community technology in washington state

Individual Benefits

- **Academic Skills and Literacy**
  - Providing references and/or resumes for college or jobs
  - Academic improvement like raising math scores one letter grade
  - Preparing users to obtain a GED or go to college

- *"I lived 27 years in the US. Over 20 years in Los Angeles. I came here; my daughter was sick. She asked for help. When I came here], I couldn't speak or understand English. I start at English level 1. Now I am at level 5. When I finish level 5, I'd like to go to college. I like to be a nurse. Soon I take my GED. I have 4 kids. I worked for my kids. Now is time for me."* La Casa Hogar, Yakima

November 30, 2007 9

communities • connect • network
advancing community technology in washington state

Individual Benefits

- **Social Inclusion and Personal Growth**
  - Relationship building/friendship
  - Staying out of trouble
  - Developing or expanding interests
  - Tangible skill development (e.g. leadership, public speaking)
  - Providing connections to community leaders
  - Building confidence and elevating expectations

- *"The CTC has helped a lot of people who thought they didn't know how to do anything, for example, one woman wanted to have a bake sale. Using the CTC, she was able to learn to use Publisher and market the sale to other residents."* Delridge Neighborhood Development Association, Seattle

November 30, 2007 10

communities • connect • network
advancing community technology in washington state

Family Benefits

- **Employment/Economic Benefits**
  - Helping users to get a better paying job

- *"One woman studied ESL. She went to school for cosmetology and then got a job." This appeared particularly significant for seasonal laborers who wished to move beyond working in the fields.* La Casa Hogar, Yakima

November 30, 2007 11

communities • connect • network
advancing community technology in washington state

Family Benefits

- **Academic Skills and Literacy**
  - Connecting families to technology
  - Ability to help school aged children

- *"Children who have participated in club media programs have their work posted online. Families often don't know anything about the Internet. Families wanted to see their kids and asked for CDs or recordings, but the staff guided them to get onto the Internet instead, and as they start going to their kids, it begins a conversation about the Internet among the family. Also, a lot of the students have grandparents as guardians, so the generation gap is large. Grandparents have started using the center to start interest groups in learning how to use these technologies."* 4-H Network News, Jefferson County

November 30, 2007 12

communities • connect • network
advancing community technology in washington state

Family Benefits

- **Social Inclusion and Personal Growth**
  - Improving family relationships
  - Keeping kids safe by checking their online activities

- *"There are two girls who look like success if you see them walking down the street. One girl's mother died when she was young. Her dad was in and out of jail. She did this documentary about her dad's relationship. It made an impact. Now, she has a relationship with her dad and it came out of her Reel Grrls experience."* Reel Grrls, Seattle

November 30, 2007 13

communities • connect • network
advancing community technology in washington state

Community Benefits

- **Employment/Economic Benefits**
  - More skilled work force
  - Better educated population

- *"all staff were former students who have moved into leadership positions"* La Casa Hogar, Yakima
- *"at least 50% of the youth have gone on to college, 10-15% work in technical fields, and the rest are still around working in technical environments. We have 13 kids working in internships and contract status this summer."* Intel Computer Clubhouse, Tacoma
- *"learn innovative software that goes beyond basic skills…and apply it to creating things that are meaningful to themselves and community." (50% of the youth are transient, 25% are homeless and all live below the poverty line).* Intel Computer Clubhouse, Tacoma

November 30, 2007 14

communities • connect • network
advancing community technology in washington state

Community Benefits

- **Social Inclusion and Personal Growth**
  - Develop future leaders
  - Motivate users to take action in their communities
  - Community building
- *"They [the clubhouse] supports them during their time there. The kids often come back to volunteer and/or give back to community. They operate under a model of service. They teach the idea of "Sankofa"- an African term for going back to get someone as you climb."* Intel Computer Clubhouse, Tacoma
- *"People share skills. We have families who don't have any exposure to technology and they learn through other residents."* Delridge Neighborhood Development Association, Seattle
- *"It is a big part of the community. It is a stepping stone between home life and public life. It bridges these two spaces of the women's lives. Culturally they aren't always comfortable with the public sphere, this bridges it. Those who know more teach those who know less. They help others."* La Casa Hogar, Yakima

November 30, 2007 15

communities • connect • network
advancing community technology in washington state

Barriers

- **Inadequate staffing or instructors**
  - *"not enough staffing. Kids must be supervised in the CTC but there are not enough people to monitor kids and give them computer access. Sometimes she's the only one there and can't supervise them in the CTC, so they can't go down there."* Delridge Neighborhood Development Association, Seattle
- **Funding issues**
  - *"It is easier to get technology funding than staff funding."* Reel Grrls, Seattle
  - *"The organization currently lacks the requisite money to replace their aging desktop and laptop computers."* Washington CASH, Seattle
- **Insufficient space, computers or technologies**
  - *"Once I wanted to study the computers, but there wasn't room"* Yesler Terrace, Seattle
  - *"It's hard to run an Internet business with no bandwidth "* Stone Soup, Republic

November 30, 2007 16

communities • connect • network
advancing community technology in washington state

Voices from the Field

- In the process of doing our research, we collected many stories from the sites we visited and surveyed that show the direct impact community technology is making in Washington State

Reel Grrls office and users' work area (small table)

- Rather than giving those to you second hand, we have here with us today people who are making all this possible
- They will give you a first hand picture of the impact, barriers and needs of community technology providers

November 30, 2007 17

communities • connect • network
advancing community technology in washington state

Our Speakers

- Peg Giffels, *NPower Seattle*
- Luversa Sullivan, *Computer Clubhouse and Evergreen State College*
- Mike Corsini, *Star Center*
- Chris Tugwell , *YMCA Metrocenter Technology Education Center*
- Ken Thompson , *Program Officer, Bill & Melinda Gates Foundation*

November 30, 2007 18

APPENDIX C

Community Technology Center Evaluation: CTC Staff Telephone Survey Guide

This telephone survey guide will be used by project investigators to collect specific information on each Community Technology Center identified in the list of subject organizations (as listed in grant application A24042). The interview is expected to last less than 10 minutes, and results will be recorded by the investigator in a Catalyst WebQ form available only to the project researchers. Screen shots of the data collection form are appended.

Hi! My name is {xxxxx}. I'm from The Information School at the University of Washington. We are studying how people use and benefit from community technology centers. We are particularly interested in such things as what type of center you operate, who uses your center, how many people you serve with your programs, why people use your services, and any significant stories you might have about your center.

The results of this study will provide us with information that will be used to shape better statewide advocacy strategies for community technology to help further sustainability. My questions will take about 10 minutes. All questions are optional and confidential.

Do you have any questions?

Would you like to participate in our study?

[If "yes," then ask: "Is this a good time for you to take the survey, or would you like to arrange another time that would be better for your schedule?" If the answer is no, then proceed with the survey and enter results in the Catalyst WebQ form. If later, ask to set up a time that will work, and provide a phone number and email address where you can be reached if a conflict arises.]

[if "no," then say "Thank you very much for your time." and end call.]

Catalyst Survey Questions

Question 1.

Please enter the interviewer's name here.

Question 2.

Please enter today's date here.

Question 3.

Please enter the CTC organization's name that is listed on the spreadsheet here.

Question 4.

Please ask the CTC organization to **verify** its name and enter it here.

Question 5.

Do you have a website for your organization? If so, what is the URL?

Question 6.

How many staff are working at your CTC?

Question 7.

What year did your CTC start?

Question 8.

Please provide the name(s) of your CTC program(s).

Question 9.

Are there any programs you would like to add in the future?

Question 10.

On average, how many people per week use your center throughout the year?

Question 11.

How many unique visitors did you have in the last year?

Question 12.

Who is your **primary** audience?

- ☐ Adults
- ☐ Disabled
- ☐ Homeless
- ☐ Immigrant
- ☐ Residents
- ☐ Youth
- ☐ Native Americans
- ☐ Low Income
- ☐ Other: ______

Question 13.

Who else uses your center? (Choose all that apply)

- ☐ Adults
- ☐ Disabled
- ☐ Immigrant
- ☐ Residents
- ☐ Youth
- ☐ Native Americans
- ☐ Low Income
- ☐ Staff
- ☐ Other: ______

Question 14.

What is your center type? (Choose all that apply)

- ☐ Senior Center
- ☐ School/College/University
- ☐ Nonprofit Organization
- ☐ Neighborhood Service Center
- ☐ Neighborhood Community Center
- ☐ Library
- ☐ Housing Complex
- ☐ For Profit Business
- ☐ Government
- ☐ Public Access Cable
- ☐ Other: ________

Question 15.

What are the top two reasons people use your center?

- ☐ Find and connect with other people or community services
- ☐ Get a job
- ☐ Communicate with family, friends and others
- ☐ Learn new job skills
- ☐ Learn new technologies or new skills
- ☐ Improve school performance
- ☐ Be a leader and help others
- ☐ Graduate from school or go to college
- ☐ Learn skills for independence
- ☐ Learn English
- ☐ Other (please specify)

Question 16.

What are the barriers to using your center? (For example, childcare or transportation?)

Question 17.

Do you have any additional comments regarding what we talked about today (success stories, special needs, unique strengths)?

Thank you for taking the time to participate in our survey. We really appreciate your contribution to the study.

About the Contributors

Jack Baur received his MLIS from the iSchool at the University of Washington in 2008 and is currently working as a teen services librarian at the Berkeley Public Library in Berkeley, California.

Esther Benson graduated with her MLIS degree from the University of Washington in August 2008 and was a member of the field research team contributing to this study.

Theresa Benson graduated with her MLIS degree from the University of Washington in June 2008 and was a member of the field research team contributing to this study. She is currently working as a family support specialist for Puget Sound Educational Service District.

Maggie Hardiman is a graduate student in the MLIS program at the University of Washington and was a member of the field research team contributing to this study.

Sophy Johnston graduated with her MLIS degree from the University of Washington in August 2008 and was a member of the field research team contributing to this study.

Rebecca Kuglitsch is the science liaison librarian at University of Puget Sound. She received her MLIS at the iSchool at the University of Washington in 2008, where she became involved with the Communities Connect Network project.

Carol F. Landry is a doctoral student at the iSchool at the University of Washington, where she is studying information behavior and the affect of emotion and time pressure on decision making. Previous to beginning her doctoral studies, Landry earned an MLIS from the Information School. As a researcher, she has investigated the information behavior of dentists and collaborated with colleagues on such studies as the information behavior of stay-at-home mothers, the information grounds of college students, and the impact of community technology centers. Currently, Landry is working on research addressing the impact of free access to computers and the internet in public libraries.

Meghan Madonna graduated with her MLIS degree from the University of Washington in June 2008 and was a member of the field research team contributing to this study.

Barbara McKnight graduated with her MLIS degree from the University of Washington in March 2009 and was a member of the field research team contributing to this study. She is an adjunct instructor in the Business Information Technology department at Edmonds Community College. Since February 2007, she has been working with North Sound 2-1-1, promoting awareness of the resource and improving the database.

Charles M. Naumer is a PhD candidate in information science at the iSchool at the University of Washington, where he is working on his dissertation on the use of "framing" as a means of sensemaking. He also holds a degree in Economics from Pomona College and a master's degree in Public Policy from the John F. Kennedy School of Government at Harvard. Naumer has spent more than 20 years working in the public, nonprofit, and private sectors, and is a founding partner of CiviCore, with a core mission of utilizing the web to provide organizations in the social sector with cost-effective, capacity-building information technology solutions. Naumer's current research interests include developing information architecture that supports sensemaking, evaluation, decision making, problem solving, and innovation within organizations. His focus has been on utilizing qualitative research methods within information systems to improve insight and organizational effectiveness.

Sonja Sutherland is a reference librarian and instructor at Valdosta State University. She teaches information literacy for undergraduates and a graduate-level course on library research methods for online students. She earned her MLIS at the University of Washington in 2008.

About the Editors

Michael Crandall is chair of the Master of Science in Information Management program and a senior lecturer in the Information School (iSchool) at the University of Washington. Prior to joining the Information School in January 2005, he spent five years as technology manager for the Bill & Melinda Gates Foundation's Libraries and Public Access to Information Program, where he was responsible for software development, technical support, and network deployment for more than 40,000 public access computers in more than 11,000 libraries across the U.S. As part of this project, Mr. Crandall also initiated and managed the program grant for development of WebJunction, an international public access computing portal. Before this, Mr. Crandall was manager of the Knowledge Architecture Group at Microsoft Information Services, responsible for design and management of the technical infrastructure and search services for Microsoft's intranet portal site, MSWeb (2.2 million requests and 31,000 users per month), and the design, development, and management of a corporate taxonomy project to support content management and retrieval throughout the company. Prior to Microsoft, he worked at the Boeing Company on multiple projects related to information management and information architecture, including an internal real-time newsfeed, the intranet search engine and portal subject access tools, and the company library's website. He was a member of the Boeing Information Management Standards Board, Web Advisory Board, Knowledge Management team, and Structured Information Objects (metadata schemas) Technical Working Group. He has served on the Dublin Core Metadata Board of Trustees since its inception in 2001 and is active in the American Society for

Information Science & Technology (ASIS&T). Research interests include impacts of public access computing, ICT in developing countries, metadata and knowledge organization, social dimensions of knowledge transfer and large-scale information systems.

Dr. Karen E. Fisher is a professor at the iSchool at the University of Washington. Dr. Fisher's teaching and research strives to answer a pertinent and persistent question of information services and information systems: "How are we making a difference in people's lives—to users, families, neighborhoods, and communities—especially in ways that speak to policy makers?" Building on the understanding that, much like an iceberg, only 20 percent of how people use systems is easily visible (and measurable) by the naked eye, Dr. Fisher advocates the use of a context-based, outcomes-centered approached for identifying the remaining 80 percent. As co-author of *How Libraries and Librarians Help* (2005), her recent work focused on community technology centers in Washington State and the new Seattle Public Library building as "Place." In 2008, she and Senior Lecturer Michael Crandall began studying the benefits of free access to computers in public libraries—an unprecedented, nationwide study supported by the Institute of Museum and Library Services and the Bill & Melinda Gates Foundation. Dr. Fisher is the co-editor of *Theories of Information Behavior* (2005) and was a Visiting Researcher at Microsoft Research in the Community Technologies Group (2006–07). Supporters of her work include the National Science Foundation, Microsoft Research, United Way of America, the Social Sciences and Humanities Research Council of Canada. Recipient of the 2005 and 2008 Jesse H. Shera Award for Distinguished Published Research from the American Library Association, Dr. Fisher has been recognized for her work by ASIS&T SIG USE and the Association for Library and Information Science Education. Dr. Fisher is a graduate of the University of Western Ontario (PhD and MLIS) and Memorial University of Newfoundland (BA), and held a postdoc at the University of Michigan.

Claire Connell (Associate Editor) works as a writer/editor for University of Washington Learning and Scholarly Technologies, where she writes and edits communications materials, research reports, and online help documentation. Ms. Connell is a PhD candidate in ethnomusicology at the University of Washington. She has presented at national and international conferences of ethnomusicology and music education, has taught a number of college-level courses, and has co-authored an article in the *Journal of Research in Music Education*. Ms. Connell also works part-time in the Education Department of the nonprofit organization Seattle Theatre Group, where she is driven by the philosophy that every student should have equal access to the arts.

Index

D

E

T

U

V

W

Y

Z

More Titles of Interest from Information Today, Inc.

Understanding and Communicating Social Informatics

A Framework for Studying and Teaching the Human Contexts of Information and Communication Technologies

By Rob Kling, Howard Rosenbaum, and Steve Sawyer

Here is a sustained investigation into the human contexts of information and communication technologies (ICTs), covering both research and theory. The authors demonstrate that the design, adoption, and use of ICTs are deeply connected to people's actions as well as to the environments in which ICTs are used. They offer a pragmatic overview of social informatics, articulating its fundamental ideas for specific audiences and presenting important research findings.

240 pp/hardbound/ISBN 978-1-57387-228-7/$39.50

Theories of Information Behavior

Edited by Karen E. Fisher, Sanda Erdelez, and Lynne (E. F.) McKechnie

This unique book presents authoritative overviews of more than 70 conceptual frameworks for understanding how people seek, manage, share, and use information in different contexts. Covering both established and newly proposed theories of information behavior, the book includes contributions from 85 scholars from 10 countries. Theory descriptions cover origins, propositions, methodological implications, usage, and links to related theories.

456 pp/hardbound/ISBN 978-1-57387-230-0
ASIST Members $39.60 • Nonmembers $49.50

Knowledge Management Lessons Learned

What Works and What Doesn't

Edited by Michael E. D. Koenig and T. Kanti Srikantaiah

A follow-up to Srikantaiah and Koenig's ground-breaking *Knowledge Management for the Information Professional*, this new book surveys recent applications and innovations in KM. More than 30 experts describe KM in practice, revealing what has been learned, what works, and what doesn't. Includes projects undertaken by organizations at the forefront of KM, and coverage of KM strategy and implementation, cost analysis, education and training, content management, communities of practice, competitive intelligence, and much more.

624 pp/hardbound/ISBN 978-1-57387-181-5
ASIST Members $35.60 • Nonmembers $44.50

Knowledge Management in Practice

Connections and Context

Edited by T. Kanti Srikantaiah and Michael E. D. Koenig

This third entry in the ambitious, highly regarded KM series from editors Srikantaiah and Koenig features 26 chapters contributed by more than 20 experts from around the globe. The book not only looks at how KM is being implemented in organizations today, but is unique in surveying the efforts of KM professionals to extend knowledge beyond their organizations and in providing a framework for understanding user context. *Knowledge Management in Practice* is a must-read for any professional seeking to connect organizational KM systems with increasingly diverse and geographically dispersed user communities.

544 pp/hardbound/ISBN 978-1-57387-312-3
ASIST Members $47.60 • Nonmembers $59.50

Information and Emotion

The Emergent Affective Paradigm in Information Behavior Research and Theory

Edited by Diane Nahl and Dania Bilal

Information and Emotion introduces the new research areas of affective issues in information seeking and use and the affective paradigm applied to information behavior in a variety of populations, cultures, and contexts. The book's editors and authors are information behavior researchers at the forefront of charting the emotional quality of the information environment. Colletively, their contributions make *Information and Emotion* a unique source of research findings on the user perspective; the user experience; and how emotional aspects can be interpreted, mitigated, or enhanced through design that is informed by use, and by users who directly participate in information design.

392 pp/hardbound/ISBN 978-1-57387-310-9
ASIST Members $47.60 • Nonmembers $59.50

Computerization Movements and Technology Diffusion

From Mainframes to Ubiquitous Computing

Edited by Margaret S. Elliott and Kenneth L. Kraemer

"Computerization movement" (CM), as first articulated by Rob Kling, refers to a special kind of social and technological movement that promotes the adoption of computing within organizations and society. Here, editors Margaret S. Elliott and Kenneth L. Kraemer and more than two dozen noted scholars trace the successes and failures of CMs from the mainframe and PC eras to the emerging era of ubiquitous computing. The empirical studies presented here show the need for designers, users, and the media to be aware that CM rhetoric can propose grand visions that never become part of a reality and reinforce the need for critical and scholarly review of promising new technologies.

608 pp/hardbound/ISBN 978-1-57387-311-6
ASIST Members $47.60 • Nonmembers $59.50